REVOLT IN SYRIA

STEPHEN STARR

REVOLT IN SYRIA

EYE-WITNESS TO THE UPRISING

Columbia University Press
New York

Columbia University Press
Publishers Since 1893
New York
cup.columbia.edu

Library of Congress Cataloging-in-Publication Data

Starr, Stephen.
Revolt in Syria : eye-witness to the uprising / Stephen Starr.
p. cm.
Includes bibliographical references and index.
ISBN 978-0-231-70420-5 (alk. paper)
1. Syria--Politics and government--2000- 2. Syria--Social condi
tions--21st century. 3. Protest movements--Syria--History--21st
century. 4. Political violence--Syria--History--21st century. 5. Starr,
Stephen--Travel--Syria. 6. Journalists--Syria--Biography. I. Title.

DS98.6.S73 2012
956.9104'2--dc23

2012022111

∞

Columbia University Press books are printed on permanent and durable
acid-free paper. This book is printed on paper with recycled content.

Printed in the USA

c 10 9 8 7 6 5 4 3 2 1

CONTENTS

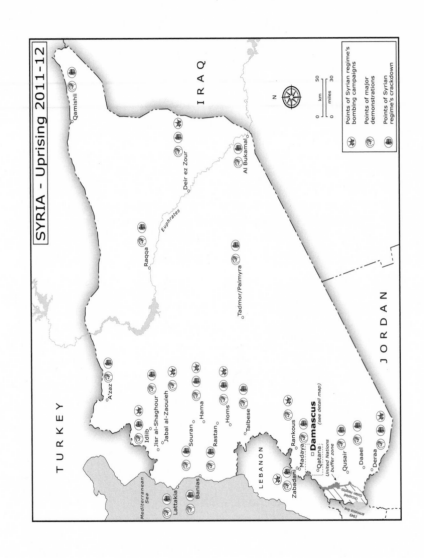

SYRIA – Uprising 2011-12

TURKEY

IRAQ

JORDAN

LEBANON

Mediterranean Sea

Euphrates

Qamishli

Deir ez Zour

Al Bukamal

Raqqa

Tadmor/Palmyra

Azaz

Idlib

Jisr al-Shaghour

Jabal al-Zaouieh

Souran

Hama

Rastan

Homs

Talbeese

Rankous

Damascus
(see detail map)

Madaya

Qatana

United Nations
buffer zone

Zabadani

Qusair

Daael

Deraa

Lattakia

Banias

Golan Heights

1949 armistice line

N

km   50
0
miles   30
0

Points of Syrian regime's
bombing campaigns

Points of major
demonstrations

Points of Syrian
regime's crackdown

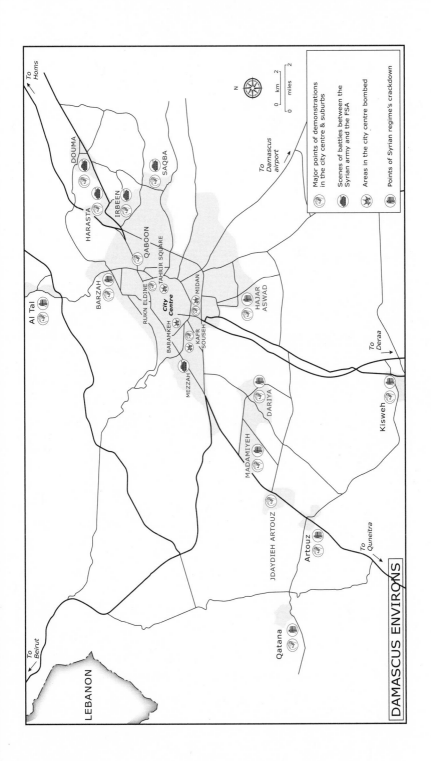

DAMASCUS ENVIRONS

Legend:

- Major points of demonstrations in the city centre & suburbs
- Scenes of battles between the Syrian army and the FSA
- Areas in the city centre bombed
- Points of Syrian regime's crackdown

N

0 km 2
0 miles 2

To Homs

To Damascus airport

To Deraa

To Qunetra

To Beirut

LEBANON

Al Tal

DOUMA

SAQBA

IRBEEN

HARASTA

QABOON

TAHRIR SQUARE

BARZAH

RUKN ELDINE

City Centre

MIDAN

HAJAR ASWAD

BARAMKEH

KAFR SOUSEH

MEZZAH

DARIYA

MADAMIYEH

JDAYDIEH ARTOUZ

Artouz

Kisweh

Qatana

PROLOGUE

Thirteen women and children have moved into my friend's summer house in Hamoryeh [east of Damascus]," an accountant told me. "He said they had nothing but the clothes on their backs. He was actually crying – not because his house was occupied, but because this is what has become of Syria."

It was early February 2012 and a series of rebellious suburbs and towns east of the capital had just fallen to regime forces.

For periods of between a few days and several weeks, rebels from the so-called Free Syria Army – mostly defected soldiers from the regular army – manned their own checkpoints and 'protected' anti-regime protests only ten kilometres from Damascus city centre.

It was an assignment to one of these suburbs that impelled me to leave Syria after almost five years.

Visiting the scenes in Saqba in eastern Damascus (see chapter VII) made me feel as if staying in the country had simply become too risky. Flying out of Damascus airport, where I was questioned for thirty minutes by an official and a military officer, and where tanks surrounded the runway, undetectable from the air, I was filled with relief and regret. I had to sell my apartment. I had to convince myself I was not being overly paranoid. I was leaving behind the news story of the year.

But elements among the myriad state security services knew where I lived, where I went each day and who my friends and acquaintances were. I had five years of roots to be pored over by the relevant authorities, if, when and how they pleased.

The regime's assault on Baba Amr and other dissenting districts of Homs in February 2012 proved a watershed moment for the revolt: had the rebels managed to fend off the regime's brutal attack and actually hold on to territory it could have convinced Syrians (and countries) eager to end the Assad regime that it was a serious, capable entity. Instead, the entire world saw Syria's armed opposition for what it was: a mostly disorganised group with limited capabilities. Neither the political or armed opposition have particularly endeared themselves to the millions of Syrians sitting on the fence or to elements of the international community keen to stop the regime's violence. Rebels fled Homs in early March after a month of intense shelling by regime forces, claiming they wanted to save civilian lives. Many Syrians wondered why they didn't leave a month before and thus spare many hundred more.

The international news circuit was shocked by the deaths of the brave journalists Marie Colvin and Remi Ochlik in Homs on 22 February 2012. But we did not hear how many Syrians were killed (seven) in the same attack. International observers should be more concerned about the stories of the fourteen activists who died attempting to smuggle Paul Conway, the photographer injured in the same shelling that killed Colvin and Ochlik, out of Homs on 28 February. The potential for radicalisation amongst their families and friends probably increased exponentially as a result, perhaps encouraging them to take up arms against the regime. Such stories have been repeated thousands of times around the country.

The Syrian army also quelled dissidence in Zabadani and Harasta around the capital, in Hama, Idlib and several other centres of protest around the country for the umpteenth time in March 2012. But they are hollow victories even as state media claim the revolt is "over". As was the case in one town that features prominently in this book, each time the army entered the town protestors quietened, but when it left again the revolutionaries and activists went back to work. They will continue to do so.

The 'pot of gold' cash injection announced at the second Friends of Syria meeting in Istanbul on 1 April smacked of Saudi Arabia and Qatar – two leading international denouncers of the regime – wishing to exert control in Syria without getting their hands dirty. The move will see the Gulf countries paying the Free Syria Army in an attempt to encourage more defections.

Saudi Arabia was never particularly popular with Syrians before March 2011 and this venture is unlikely to increase further defections (soldiers and officers who may wish to defect are more concerned with staying alive than with promises of bounties). Kofi Annan, the Arab League and UN special envoy to Syria succeeded in getting the regime to agree to an 10 April 2012 deadline for the partial implementation of a proposed peace plan. This plan would see a ceasefire monitoring mission deployed to Syria, the withdrawal of the regime's military forces from urban centres and permission for humanitarian aid to enter the areas most affected by the violence. At the time of writing, the makeup of such a force has not been discussed but it is likely the regime will adopt the same plan it did for the visit of the failed Arab League observer mission.

The Syrian deputy oil minister who defected to the opposition on 7 March counted as the highest ranking government official in a year of revolt, remarkably. Rather than serving as a reflection of a regime crumbling, this was more a reminder of just how tough a nut to crack it has been after a full year of revolt.

The regime has no interest in peace, only in keeping power. As with past plans, it will use this chapter to carry out further crackdowns. Thus far, it has successfully faced down the international community which once proposed UN resolutions calling for Assad to step down. It routed the rebels in Baba Amr, Idlib and elsewhere around the country in February and March 2012. On a certain level, it has never felt stronger and more convinced it can win than it does in April 2012. But perhaps this arrogance will lead to its ultimate downfall.

Conversations among Syrians continue to run in circles. "Everyone has the right to be free and to say what he wants," one would say. "Free to do what – to destroy shops in the name of freedom because they hate Bashar al-Assad? This is not freedom," went the reply over coffee and cigarettes all over the country time and time again. This is perhaps the most worrisome aspect I have observed during the revolt. Today in Syria people are cast and characterised as being either with or against the regime. Children go around the school yard asking each other this question, where the seeds of a new divided generation are budding. The space for discussion and debate that flourished as the revolt spread last spring has unfortunately been lost as the death count rises and as people are forced to take sides.

The Assad regime has cleverly and devastatingly initiated civil conflict, but it is the 22 million Syrians who decide to continue or end it. The regime has fooled many and proved incredibly durable. But we should not be surprised (a surprise initiated by the previous successful Arab revolts of 2011): the entire political and security system, and by consequence, Syrian society, have been built with this moment of internal revolt in mind. Hafez al-Assad was a master strategist.

On the ground, in many parts of Syria life continues almost as normal. Schools remain open, millions of state employees are still being paid every month. In Damascus and Aleppo, where almost half the country's population live, people have tired of the power cuts and rising prices.

Many Damascenes dream of the old days; they hold the regime in contempt, but desire regular electricity supply, stable prices and normality more than the freedom that their countrymen fight for both north and south of them. Revolt fatigue is affecting millions of people. The majority of Syrians will not take to the streets in protest because they do not have electricity or because food has risen in cost. Most will only take to the streets when a relative or loved one has been killed by the regime.

In the long term the regime simply cannot win this fight. Too many have suffered too much. But nor can the opposition win outright in the near future.

Syria seems set for months and perhaps years of economic stagnation, brutal repression and divisions.

Stephen Starr
Ireland, April 2012

INTRODUCTION

"On Friday mornings we go to areas where there will be protests. We wait for them to come out of the mosques. We try to get by the security checkpoints, the shooting and then get the injured to ambulances. If we get that far we then have to treat the injured, or pronounce them dead and give them back to their families. While we do all this we have to avoid the bullets and get out past the checkpoints without being detained. We are caught in the middle. We are trying to help people; the injured; the dead. But in a situation like ours being in the middle is almost impossible."

These are the words of Mohammad, a worker at the Red Crescent in Damascus, as told to me in November 2011, eight months into Syria's bloody uprising. "Many workers and volunteers in the Red Crescent quit their jobs and stayed at home. Others quit their jobs and took to the streets and protested. Me? I am stuck between trying to save lives and my friends who are on the run."

Mohammad could not sit for long or say too much as he felt a "net tightening" around him, a reference to the omnipresence of the security apparatus. He said he had done nothing wrong but that his friends and colleagues who had begun protesting had been detained and might have given his name to the security services. Mohammad told me of how one colleague was killed and three others injured recently when a Red Crescent ambulance was fired upon approaching a checkpoint in Homs. He had been to the funeral the week before we spoke.

The impossible work being attempted by Mohammad and his colleagues reflected the broader complexity and difficulties that faced Syrians throughout the 2011–12 revolt, an uprising that saw thousands die and tens of thousands more beaten and tortured. Some Syrians called for President Bashar al-Assad's execution, others for his deification. Internal support for and opposition to the revolt meant that this episode of the wider Arab awakenings was the bloodiest and longest.

For a long time Syria has been a country more feared than understood. A police state with links to Iran and ill-regarded by most in the western political world, it is, nevertheless, known to those who have visited it for its famous hospitality, sumptuous food and spectacular ancient sites. Those who stay longer are familiar with the intricacies of the country's religious make up, the taboo topics and the economic difficulties being faced by the vast majority. Very few know of Syria's complex social make up or how Syrians lived and thought as the country teetered on the brink of civil war following the 2011 revolt.

When I first arrived in Damascus, I worked as an editor for *Syria Times*, a state-run newspaper that was not so much a publication of news but an anti-America, anti-Israel pamphlet. I was keen to learn more about the country and, at the time, it was to me a job in writing. All the news we received was controlled and we were not allowed to write about anything that might not be in line with conventional wisdom – try as I did. Most of the employees of the newspaper, which shared office space with the Arabic newspaper *Tishreen*, were not actually journalists, but a nephew or daughter of someone important, usually from the ruling Alawite sect.

I learned that Syrian society is a complex mix of religions, cultures and ideals. About 75 per cent of the population are Sunni Muslims, while 15 per cent consist of other Muslim sects, including Shia, Druze, Alawite and Ismaili. Of the Christians – roughly 10 per cent of the population – there are Orthodox (of various forms), Catholic, Maronite and Syriac, with a small Protestant element.

The average monthly wage amounts to about US$300 and, even before the uprising, gas, diesel and petrol, as everywhere, were becoming expensive. While the people are welcoming and friendly, I learned that talking about the government or politics or even religion was not something Syrians do with a stranger: many people earned long prison sentences for as little as publicly calling for elections or political change.

INTRODUCTION

On the street, I found out that giving a tightly-folded fifty Syrian lira note (about one dollar) to the nearest policeman could get you anything from a double-parking space for twenty minutes to instant forgiveness for running a red light. For the younger generation, it is the embedded corruption that is most frustrating. From being accepted into a good school to getting good grades to getting a reasonable job, you must have an uncle or brother to cultivate your interests. The (at the time) twenty-one months of compulsory military training distressed and further depressed thousands of young men. Whether your 'service' was spent guarding the gates of the university's language school or washing and rewashing a twenty-five-year-old Mercedes owned by your commanding general also depended on who your friends in power were.

For the people in the Jazeera and Houran areas of eastern and southern Syria – two of the country's breadbasket regions – a debilitating drought that began in 2008 saw the forced movement of around 300,000 farmers and labourers to cities such as Aleppo, Damascus and Deraa. In the Syrian capital, I would regularly be asked by taxi drivers to direct them to my destination. When asked why they didn't know the area in question, they would tell me they were from Deir Ez Zour or Hassake and had come to Damascus for work, sharing a single taxi with perhaps four other drivers, owned by another who paid them the bare minimum.

However, with increased access to money in parts of the country from 2008 and especially in urban centres I found that people were largely content. Laptop computers had been a common sight in the restaurants and cafés of the capital from 2009 and open borders with some neighbouring countries, especially Turkey, led to a sense of development and achievement taking hold of the new, post-Hafez generation Syrians.

The seed that initiated protests in Syria was innocuous enough. In early March 2011, a number of youths in the southern city of Deraa, imitating what they had seen in Tunisia and Egypt, wrote anti-government graffiti on the walls of a school. They were caught by the school principal and the *mukhabarat*, or security services, were called. The youths were taken into custody. Their fingernails were pulled out and they were beaten. When the mothers of the children approached the local police to ask for their return they were told, "You won't be getting your children back. Go home and tell your useless husbands to make you some more." Several of the youths' parents were from prominent local families and two mothers went into the streets with some other relatives to protest against the internment of their children. They too were arrested and it was from there that Syria's uprising took root. Ten days later a small group of human rights activists protested in the main market of Souk Hamadiyeh in Damascus, seeking the release of those arrested in Deraa and nationwide political reforms – a long-term demand of theirs. Each individual at the march were seized by security forces and detained. Then, three days later, on 18 March, a friend of a friend who knew I was a journalist called me. It was a Friday and I was stuck in the city centre of Damascus amid hundreds of thousands of pro-regime demonstrators. The girl, whom we will call Noor, called me from Deraa and was hysterical: "You have to do something. There are dozens of people lying dead on the streets around me," she said, barely able to speak. Noor had returned to her home town of Deraa the day before from Damascus, where she was studying English literature, to be with her family as tensions in the town escalated. "You need to report this and tell people in other countries what is happening. I can't believe this is happening. There are bodies on the ground. I need to get away from the square and go hide." I did not know what to say to her, other than to ask a couple of factual questions. I was sure my phone was being tapped. I went to the nearest internet point – a restaurant in the Bab Touma area – and filed what was happening in front of me to the *Los Angeles Times*.

Later that night, I saw on Al Jazeera television the grainy, impossible images of a statue of the former president, Hafez al-Assad, being hauled down by a dozen men in Noor's town. It was an incredible sight to behold. Before the uprising, I would lie awake at night thinking of stories to pitch to editors. I thought of the major headlines, the impossible outcomes: an invasion by Israel, a bombing campaign by Islamists, maybe even a visit by an American president. But this scene, in which these young Syrians were destroying perhaps the country's chief symbol of authority, which had up to then commanded such respect, was hardly believable.

The anti-government uprisings that swept the four corners of the country were unprecedented in the history of modern Syria. They were also completely unexpected. In late January, President Bashar al-Assad confidently told journalists from the *Wall Street Journal* that because he was close to his people, his rule was "immune" to the same troubles that had seen long-standing dictators fall by the wayside in Egypt, Libya, Tunisia and Yemen, and had led to serious unrest in Bahrain. By the time anti-government protests had spread to other parts of the country – Lattakia and Banias by early April – the authorities had set in motion a plan to destroy the growing movement of dissent.

The protests forced the regime's hand. It had to choose between grasping a new future and reverting to the violent tactics that had worked so well under the previous president, albeit in a very different time. In a massive miscalculation, it chose the latter. During the uprising the government fought back with an elaborate propaganda campaign, deploying thousands onto the streets of Damascus to demonstrate in support of President Assad. In addition, a number of major concessions were announced which served to placate the millions in Syria's two largest cities, Aleppo and Damascus.

On 30 March, two weeks after the outbreak of protests, the president's first speech to parliament since 2007 saw him announce the end of emergency laws which had been in place since 1963. This meant – in theory – an end to arrest and detention without a warrant from relevant authorities and that, for anyone arrested, an appearance in front of a judge was a legal right, rather than the detainee being taken, locked up and never heard of again, as had happened thousands of times in the past. Hundreds of political prisoners were released. Around 300,000 Kurds were to be granted Syrian citizenship, people who had been stateless and without basic rights since moving from Turkey in the 1920s.

But these words were contradicted almost at once. The army took decisive steps. The tanks were called into trouble spots around the country, one by one, in a full-scale military assault.

How did I succeed in operating as a journalist as the unrest unfolded around Syria? I cannot answer this question satisfactorily, but there was a series of measures I took to promote my longevity in what was, by many standards, a privileged position.

I was upfront with the government. I registered as a journalist with the appropriate authorities. I plagued officials with requests for interviews, permission slips and journalist papers. I regularly called into the Ministry for Information to pick up discarded copies of English newspapers. They knew who I was; security forces had come to my home and when they did I gave them direct answers. The newspaper for which I registered myself with the Syrian authorities was an Irish business title and, six months into the revolt, thankfully erected a pay wall on its website.

I also kept a routine. When entering towns cut off by checkpoints I would do so on the same days (Fridays, thankfully), at the same time and with the same people. Security forces were told I was a language teacher. I rarely associated with foreigners, who were subjected to heightened security attention during the revolt. I changed email addresses weekly and passwords daily. I never risked speaking about certain items on the phone. I had over years come to recognise secret police on the street; how they looked, what they wore, what their body language said. This helped me make decisions on topics of conversations and when to speak English and when to use Arabic when they were close by. I got out when I felt it was time, when I had taken risks that crossed a line.

Unlike me, most Syrians could not leave their country as revolt slipped into civil strife and divisions grew. But here are their stories.

I

DAMASCUS: DRAGGED TOWARDS REVOLT

On consecutive Fridays in the spring of 2011 I watched and listened as word trickled in of small protests in villages and towns around the capital. The towns of Madamiyeh and Douma were the principal centres of unrest close to the capital at the time. But as the weeks dragged on, as people buried their dead, as the arrests and beatings and repression became more widespread, these protests mushroomed from village to village and from town to town.

Madamiyeh is a five-minute drive on the highway from the leafy Mezzah neighbourhood in south west Damascus. In Madamiyeh, a largely conservative area with a scattering of Alawites among a predominantly Sunni population, one can rent a three-bedroom apartment for a mere US$200 a month. (In Mezzah one can pay up to US$2,000 for a similar space.) When pro-regime Syrians, still on a high from the euphoria of a city centre rally, sped out along Mezzah highway and through Madamiyeh waving pictures of Bashar al-Assad one afternoon in late March, tempers flared. When it happened a second time shots were fired, regime supporters and locals were injured and then killed; thereafter the funerals of locals in the town evolved into demonstrations. Finally, the security and army moved in. It would become the scene of internments, police brutality and death. As elsewhere, it would never be free, nor fully coerced. Blood had been spilt and, as locals often told me, Syrian blood was expensive.

For the duration of the unrest I passed by this town, from its northern and southern borders, on an almost daily basis as it experienced the same crackdown as dozens of other dissenting towns. Soldiers patrolled every alleyway, demanding identification from each person to walk by. Tanks pointed their cannons inward over the town, towards homes and children. When I passed in the local microbus – a twelve-seater minibus and the preferred means of transport in Syria – each passenger around me would stare over their shoulders into the town in fear and, perhaps, pity.

Nineteen kilometres north of Damascus on the Homs highway – the central artery linking Syria's north and south – the town of Douma, famous for its production of camel meat, also became an early lightning rod for anti-regime protests. Here, too, the population could not be defied.

In the capital Damascus, however, life continued almost as normal during the spring, summer and autumn of 2011. The heart of the Sunni business class, and traditionally the last to become entangled in the mire of revolt, residents watched events in other parts of the country with much concern, but also with a feeling that the scenes being broadcast on their televisions could not be repeated there.

Throughout the wider Arab revolutions, Damascenes were glued to the Arab television networks Al Jazeera and Al Arabiya. The former, a Qatar-based news network, had long been a popular viewing choice by millions of Syrians for its coverage of the Palestinian issue, and for covering with such detail the revolutions in Tunisia, Egypt and Libya that most Syrians wholeheartedly supported. There were dozens of jokes circulating among Damascenes during the North African uprisings. One saw former Tunisian president Zine El Abidine Ben Ali waiting at his Saudi villa for both Mubarak and Gaddafi to join him to make up the numbers for a card game. Al Jazeera's pro-Arab editorial stance and swathe of correspondents in Libya, Egypt and elsewhere were doing great work in the eyes of Damascenes in uncovering the corruption and oppression that had stymied the citizens of North Africa for decades.

However, once the Doha-based organisation turned to the unfolding events in Syria many switched off out of fear or disbelief. Syrians had long been proud that, while Palestine, Lebanon and Iraq burned around them, their country was an oasis of tranquility and stability.

But as word seeped in from the countryside and as videos mushroomed on Facebook and YouTube, both of which had been legalised in the country in February 2011, Damascenes began to fear the worst. From mid-April, traffic on the streets, normally noisy and crowded, was notably absent. Cafés and restaurants, usually brim full of young men watching the latest Champion's League football game, were almost empty. After dark the streets were largely deserted. There was talk of the state exams, due in June, being postponed until September. Families withdrew funds from their bank accounts and exchanged their Syrian lira for dollars and euros. For almost five years, the conversion rate had stood at around forty-seven Syrian lira to the US dollar but by March 2012, and despite government attempts to maintain monetary stability, it topped one hundred lira to the dollar. Office desks and classrooms were empty as teachers and employees from the flashpoint satellite towns of Douma and Madamiyeh failed to show up.

But by early summer, the Damascenes, or *Shuwam* as they are known locally, as before, held on in the hope that their own riches and belongings would not come under attack. People in towns throughout Syria were being shot at by snipers, had no food to eat and were locked up in their homes. But the Damascene elite, in their fear, ignored all around them.

One Christian girl living in the capital to whom I spoke in late April 2011 echoed the official state line, saying she believed the anti-regime demonstrations were the creation of a foreign plot. "I went home to my village in Bsier [in Deraa province] for Easter, we didn't see anything. The army is there to protect the people. They waved us through checkpoints and said 'hello'." Her statement reflects a point of view common among the country's Christian community – one of denial – but also reflects the scale of division between urban and rural.

Another woman from Abbasiyeen square in northern Damascus, close to where demonstrators attempted to enter the capital from the restive town of Douma in the first week of April, said that people came over from Douma "to our doors and asked us to take to the streets. They wanted us to go and march to the square all together, like they did in Egypt. No one from my building moved, everyone was too afraid. We were simply too afraid of the regime."

During the first three months of the revolt no one went out. In late April, a decision was made by school authorities to end the primary and secondary school day at 12 noon amid falling student numbers. One Friday evening in mid-May I went for a drink at the Carlton Hotel which overlooked a security complex that was later partly destroyed in a bombing. The hotel bar was completely empty. "Things are quiet now because of the situation," said the barman serving me. Not a single guest or visitor passed through the hotel's doors in the two hours I spent there.

The Old City's two most popular hotels, which had been booked up until the end of the year and had enjoyed thriving business for several years, were now empty and had to lay off almost their entire staff. Syria's tourism industry had been worth around US$8 billion in 2010, said international reports. By early summer the following year, and after a ten-year push to reform its image, the country's economy lay in ruins.

A suit maker in the shopping area of Shalaan in the city centre averred that the situation was more complex: "Everyone wants change but it takes time. If someone comes into my shop and asks for a suit to be made, and when I don't have it right away, he breaks up my shop. Is this reasonable? Things take time in Syria."

During my work for the *Washington Post* I witnessed and reported on the troops and half a dozen tanks that I saw in the Damascus suburb of Madamiyeh. Roadblocks on the highway to the Golan Heights were erected. On the same stretch of highway, seventeen kilometres from Damascus, I witnessed a mix of soldiers, police and security officers control access to a local mosque in Artouz each Friday afternoon during the early weeks of the unrest. Their batons, their guns and their numbers meant hundreds of worshippers would file in and out of Friday prayers without shouting for freedom as they had done on previous weeks in April.

Back in Damascus, the sense of fear that first descended on the capital during the first few weeks evolved into a feeling of uneasiness. Cafés slowly filled up and more cars returned to the city's streets.

People began to go about their daily lives but business activity took a major hit. Accountants were sitting idly in offices as taxes were not being paid and sales were devastated. The owner of a car importing company explained to me that he was running out of money to pay his employees. News that over 200 members of the Baath party had resigned in protest against the shootings of protesters also unsettled many. With one hand the authorities, through their newspapers and radio and television broadcasts, were saying nothing was happening, that the country was fine. But with the other they were firing mayors and security officials when people in Deraa died. What were people to believe?

There was much fear but no action. People in Damascus have too much to lose, I was told by many friends. "They have cars, businesses, they have a healthy life. They know people are dying in other parts of the country but they are thinking of themselves," said one city resident who, like most, asked for anonymity when speaking to me.

On the streets of the capital, state newspapers portrayed images of dead security personnel and soldiers, murdered by "unknown armed gangs". SANA, the state-run news agency, reported how it had uncovered "distortion campaigns against Syria" which were led by Al Jazeera, Al Arabiya and the BBC. The pro-government news organisation said, "Such campaigns, however, are never [going] to weaken the Syrians nor shake their strong convictions or morale." People were to be against the international Arab media but were not to be afraid, so said the authorities.

A sense of disbelief among the *Shuwam* was clear, and the incessant television, radio and print reports forced upon people the idea that Syria was under threat from foreign forces and armed gangs. The propaganda proved to be remarkably successful.

Real signs of unrest in the capital, however, began to appear when around 500 people marched one Friday in April in the Midan area of the city and began shouting pro-freedom slogans.

Midan is located south of the Old City and has been known for its conservatism and wealth over a period of centuries. The city's best local restaurants are to be found here, where sheep brain, tongue and stomach, as well as camel meat, are the main attraction for Gulf tourists and locals. Back in the 1920s and 1930s Midan grew to notoriety for producing several of the country's leading anti-colonial figures, martyrs who died in the name of the Syrian people.

According to *The Economist*, the sheikh of the al-Hassan mosque in Midan, Krayyem Rajjha, a respected Islamic scholar, is a long-time critic of the government and has refused to pray for the president. On Fridays preceding the revolt, his sermons annoyed authorities for their focus on economic hardship and the *mukhabarat*. The mosque was also the site where Riad Seif, a veteran opposition figure, was arrested on 6 May, further fuelling Midan's unrest.

So why did Midan, a wealthy and conservative area in the heart of the capital, see dissent? To find out why, I went back to speak to Noor from Deraa, whose Damascus home was in the same area and close to the southern bypass at the al-Hassan mosque. We met over juice and espresso at a local café, and were equally nervous. She asked me to turn off my phone. She started her sentences in English but finished them in Arabic and there was a certain excitement in her eyes as she told me of new stories from Deraa. She was adamant that she and others she knew wanted an end to the regime. Noor then turned her phone back on to show me videos of men – state employees most likely – swinging sticks in practice for beating demonstrators. She said she took the video from the balcony of her own house in Midan. The video then moved to a line of men queuing up in front of a portakabin, waiting to be paid for their day's work against the protesters in the city's suburbs. "This is enough," she said. "Enough for the people who saw this happening in plain daylight to convince them the authorities are against the people."

***

On 30 March I went for coffee with a friend at a city centre café. All was calm, from inside the café, at least. Foreign Arabic language students played a piano, young Damascenes smoked and worked on their laptops. My friend, who I cannot name, arrived with car keys and iPhone in hand.

"Firstly, be careful of Facebook. They are all over it."

"How do you know this?" I asked.

"I posted a video of some people being beaten a few weeks ago. My uncle, who is in the Syrian parliament, called me with a message from people up high. They told him 'If you want your family to stay clean, don't have that guy posting these videos on Facebook again.'"

Outside the café, cars began to speed by; Syrian flags out their windows, beeping and shouting their support for Bashar. It struck me that very few of the women in the demonstrating cars wore the hijab, or the Islamic headscarf. In fact, the women were not Sunni or Shia, who sometimes wear the headscarf, but instead were Alawite, a liberal Muslim sect largely drawn from the coastal area. Alawites are also of the same sect as President Bashar al-Assad. These pro-regime demonstrations were sectarian. The Sunni and Shia populations of Damascus were not out supporting the government. It was the Alawites – those who had most to lose should the regime fall.

The pro-regime demonstrations in Mezzah on 25 March and across the city on 30 March were, in their most basic senses, exercises in mass self-delusion.

A foreboding atmosphere took over the city during these weeks in an outpouring of pro-Assad indulgence not seen in the country for decades. It was frankly frightening to see people I knew and thought of as friends for years behaving in such a way. Approaching people in general conversation towards the beginning of the unrest was always a tricky practice. But, after a few weeks, it became clear from the rhetoric developed that it was Saad Hariri, Bandar Bin Sultan (a Saudi prince) and the Salafists who were responsible for the unrest taking place in the rural parts of the country – it was not the government. Syria was transforming into the state of control portrayed in George Orwell's *1984*.

The state commandeered the nation's radio stations and played nationalistic songs from morning to night. Other stations held long-winded discussions about how foreigners do not know anything about Syria and shouldn't have the temerity to interfere in the country's interests. We heard over and over of the "armed terrorist groups" shooting police and soldiers across the country. In the Old City, shopkeepers competed to see who could blare out their nationalistic songs the loudest.

One evening during the wave of incongruity, as I took a microbus home, I passed the Al Jazeera offices on Mezzah highway in the south east of the capital. An employee of the network stared uneasily out of a second-storey window at the crowds below – crowds chanting for the network to leave the country and threatening to storm the building.

As we drove on amid the crowds, youths held out badly-made signs reading "BBC, Al Jazeera, Al Arabiya get out". A middle-aged woman delirious with pride, anger and insolence sat on her car window screaming "God, Syria and Bashar, only". Her eyes were wide open, a great smile on her face interjected with expressions of rage. She waved a Syrian flag over her head. Children as young as five years old were now standing in the middle of the highway – accompanied by their school teachers – screaming the same chant. No car could pass without seeing how much Syrians loved Bashar.

For about a week in March these organised and frankly bizarre rallies continued. The following Saturday afternoon in March, I spotted a cameraman for the Lebanese LBC television network being attacked while filming a pro-Assad grouping on Mezzah highway. Before long one could count the number of journalists in the city with one hand. AP, Reuters, the BBC, Al Jazeera and others either pulled out or saw their reporters forced to leave Syria.

For about a week during this period, each and every bus in the city was draped in posters portraying the president. Interestingly, almost all disappeared within the space of about twenty-four hours. Why, I wondered, did they vanish in such a uniform and timely fashion? Surely there was no direction from the authorities to take them down, surely the government wanted to maintain the image in people's minds for as long as possible. Did this mean drivers took them down at the first opportunity they had – in itself an act of defiance? If they did, this tells us that people put them up only because they were ordered to – not because they wanted to express genuine loyalty and support for the regime.

Conspicuous security vehicles, previously ridiculed for being thirty or more years old, were replaced with gleaming new BMWs, Volkswagen Passats and Honda Accords. I suspect that many more than me were surprised at the timing of this new fleet, and that the security services actually possessed such fancy cars.

Damascus University students from the Kurdish regions up north, and from Deraa and Banias, held a protest on campus in April but were swiftly arrested and beaten up by the security apparatus. For months afterwards, entry to all faculties of the university meant having to display a student card to one of several goons armed with machine guns at the university entrance gates. The university demographics had changed overnight – dozens of middle-aged men were sitting on benches around the English literature faculty in surveillance of all and waiting to pick up on any scent of protest.

Other spurious handouts were offered by the state. Syria's two mobile phone networks – Syriatel (owned by a cousin of the president) and the South Africa-based MTN – gave customers sixty minutes' free talk time at the beginning of April as a "gift from the president". This philanthropic gesture only served to crash both networks for two whole days and make all communications with the towns and areas under fire around the country impossible. Perhaps that was their intention.

The religious conservative elements were appeased when the government announced on 6 April that female teachers wearing the niqab would be allowed to return to the classrooms following a ban introduced in September 2010. In another attempt to win over the population, the price of diesel was reduced by 25 per cent on 24 May.

A savvier, less crude, media campaign started in May in a bid to draw in the educated Damascene classes. The hundreds of billboards brandishing embarrassingly large photos of the president's face were quickly replaced with messages that would be taken seriously by the Damascus public for the simple reason that they expressed an opinion that was more balanced, more in touch with the reality of the time: "With freedom comes responsibility" and "Yes to a shared life".

A number of what had been semi-independent daily publications turned firmly in favour of the authorities. Some tiptoed through the revolt, while others simply ignored what was going on.

Newspapers like *Baladna* (in both Arabic and English and independent to the extent that they were not published directly by the regime) published full front page photos of destroyed cars in the northern city of Lattakia, and claimed "terrorist groups" had been responsible for the destruction. Other newspapers published images of men and children lying injured in hospital beds. These Syrians, it was alleged, were the victims of "outside forces keen to sow instability in the country".

Simultaneously, Syrian state television was trawling the countryside looking to interview grocery shoppers in Idlib, Tartous and Lattakia, who were keen to express to the camera how peaceful and quiet things were.

It was clear the regime had been planning for this event for decades. It was obvious it was ready.

Days of uncertainty dragged into weeks and that spring protests proliferated in Deraa to become daily events. A couple of months earlier, when unrest began to break out in other areas of the north, a presidential adviser, Bouthaina Shabaan, let it be known that Bashar al-Assad was to give a speech outlining a wave of reforms for the country. The 30 March speech would break with the past, to facilitate a new future for Syria. It was to be an open address in front of the Syrian parliament, but directed to all Syrians. In reality, however, it turned out to be a body blow for the immediate future of the country. Syrians believed he had little to say other than to proclaim the end of the feared decades-old emergency laws – which meant taking powers from the myriad security forces – because of the situation unfolding in parts of the country, in order to calm the population and to end the swelling pockets of protest that had, originally, nothing to do with Bashar al-Assad. As the president spoke that morning a scattering of yellow taxis were the only signs of life on the streets of Damascus. People listened via radio, or television in grocery shops. Offices saw people gather around television sets for the speech as work was suspended for the forty minutes of his broadcast. For my part, I was entirely taken by surprise at the degree of interest Damascenes showed in what the president had to say. His previous speech to parliament was back in 2007, but he regularly appeared on television clips and in state-run newspapers. His image is omnipresent on the streets of each and every Syrian city. But this time, people were crying out for words of comfort from the president.

When he had finished his speech, the millions sitting around television sets sat back, startled by the fact that nothing had really been discussed at all. Most had expected the announce-ment of a wide range of changes, an admission of regret for the deaths in Deraa in the south and in Lattakia on the northern coast. It did not happen. A golden opportunity to unite the coun-try behind him and to introduce a new future passed by. It was a sad day for Syria.

Why did Assad shrink from change? Was it a result of being surrounded by teams of 'yes men' for the past ten years? In Jan-uary he had claimed to the *Wall Street Journal* that he was in touch with the needs of the people. This claim was difficult to corroborate on the streets of the capital as the city went back to work that Wednesday afternoon.

The killing of protesters continued to spread in the days and weeks following Assad's speech, and he was to give another, more poignant, sermon to his new government in mid-April. But by then the damage the security forces had inflicted on the Syr-ian psyche meant that his words of change, his recognition of corruption and his desire for dialogue with the Syrian people fell on deaf ears.

***

On a cloudy day in mid-May, twenty-four hours after a mass grave was uncovered close to Deraa in the south, I called a close friend to organise a meeting to talk about the situation. Samir, a twenty-eight-year-old dentist from Damascus, met me at the faculty of English in Damascus University. He was working on renovating his family's villa high in the mountains that separate Syria from Lebanon. When Samir had finished his French class we drove off into the open spaces outside Damascus.

Passing along the Barada River, whose icy mountain waters flow through the heart of Damascus each spring, we sped past green grass, trees and men barbecuing chicken on the side of the road. Over half an hour we ascended towards the mountains west of the capital. We passed the site of the Battle of Maysaloon where, in July 1920, a ragtag assemblage of Syrian soldiers and locals were defeated by the advancing French army. The battle went down in history as the bravest Syria fought in its resistance to European colonialism. We passed Ein al-Fijeh and climbed further upwards towards Samir's village. When we reached this beautiful country hamlet all was quiet, save for the braying of donkeys and chirping of blackbirds.

The purpose of Samir's work typified his spirit, roots and respect for his country. He spoke several languages, having studied in Europe, and drove his own US$55,000 4x4. However, he was aware of his privilege and said he wanted to give back to his country. "This is the best way I can show my patriotism," he told me of his efforts to develop his village. Samir had published a book of writings and was working on a project to build a community centre in the village. "The people here don't need to learn English or French, but I feel this is something I can do to raise some kind of awareness about the outside world," he said, puffing on a cigarette.

We arrived and sat down to talk about the situation. I wanted to know what this wealthy man had to say about the Damascenes and what they were saying amongst themselves. He was one of them, and I knew him well enough to trust his word.

"There are so many people; almost all people are related to the regime in some form. Their interests are tied up in the government, whether they have political links or not," he began.

"This is the revolution of the poor. In the large cities, like in Aleppo and Damascus they have interests. If there is change it's OK but they won't participate. For example, a guy like me, I'm always for justice but in my case I don't have to participate in the anti-regime protests."

"So you are saying that the business elite would prefer a change in government, but only if it means their own interests are not affected?" I asked.

"The rich would prefer change but not to the extent that it means civil war," he replied, as he readied his family gazebo for a second coat of paint.

An electrician, brought in from Damascus, fussed around him with wires and tools. On the other side of the villa the guard, or *natur,* and the guard's wife, both of whom lived full-time in a small area underneath the villa, were cleaning.

After an hour we drove back down the mountain to eat falafel sandwiches from a store in Ein al-Fijeh and he continued.

"If there is change they, the wealthy, will be afraid," he said.

"In the 1960s, when nationalisation took place, it destroyed the business class across the country," he added, referring to the economic nationalisation of all Syrian companies and industries amid a wave of socialist sentiment and an unsuccessful attempt at union with Egypt.

"The people who were affected then are still around – the memory of losing almost everything is still fresh for them and when we see the things happening now across the country that memory is stirred up again," he told me.

Samir was from a well-connected family whose father divided his time between the Gulf and Syria, and he told me of his disdain for the Damascene elite of a similar age to him who spend most of their time circling the city streets in expensive cars. Samir is well-travelled and he had plans to improve his country. His assessment of why the Damascenes had stayed largely quiet during the uprising was remarkably short and to the point: money and power are what the Damascene families care about.

As we left the village, clouds gathered overhead and claps of thunder rolled across the sky. "The weather this year has been the strangest for over ten years," the electrician told me. "Maybe someone or something from above is watching what is happening here," he added in a coded message. I didn't take up the topic. It was too risky as he already knew I was a foreigner.

Rain and hailstones the size of cherries began to spill down in a sort of Messianic display. Someone, somewhere, was angry, we mused, heading back down to the city.

"Damascenes have for centuries regarded the country folk who live in the villages around the capital as being either weak or stupid," an accountant friend told me as I tried to break through to the *Shami* or Damascus mindset. "The Damascenes have developed their own accent; they have dropped a letter of the Arabic alphabet. They have been the money, the business and the elite of the country, even of the Middle East region, for centuries. Even as the state squandered away fortunes and destroyed the country's economy in the 1970s, 80s and 90s the Damascenes continued to prosper. On top of this, they are very proud," he went on.

But surely a single point of view could not represent the inhabitants of the entire city, I thought.

Close family ties, a tradition that goes back centuries in Syria, means that extended members of families meet weekly, or even more often, something which encourages the adoption of group perspectives.

For example, the city's jewellers and goldsmiths are a closely connected group of Armenian Christians, who also deal with currency exchange. Syria's Armenian community, perhaps only eclipsed by the greater Christian community in its efforts to maintain union, are a well-educated group. They send their children to Lebanon to study in Armenian-speaking schools and they continue to maintain the rhetoric that they have been greatly wronged by a succession of Turkish governments. To a lesser extent they are angry with the Syrian authorities at home for not fully addressing the wrongs of the Ottoman Empire. During the Armenian Genocide of 1915–16 thousands of Armenians were murdered and buried in mass graves close to the eastern Syrian city of Deir Ez Zour

The same may be said for those similarly close-knit communities in Deraa, Banias, Homs and all the areas of the country that felt the brutality of the state first-hand. The end result is a greater gap between the protesting and the fearful wealthy.

"Of course the people in Damascus care about what is happening in Deraa and other places," said Samir on our way back down the mountain.

I countered that because of tribal norms, the people of Damascus did not care much for the poor communities in the countryside.

"That's not true," he said. "They care, we care but everyone is afraid."

I asked Samir, if the Damascenes had to choose between their properties and wealth and standing up for those in Deraa and Banias, which would they pick?

"They would want to help the people – they are Syrians, we are Syrians, we would help."

But why then were they not doing anything? I asked.

"There's something you need to understand," he said. "Everyone in Damascus has had to do a lot of work, paying people off, making friends, hosting parties and so forth in order to get where they are now – wherever they are. The system of *wasta* [contacts and influence] and corruption was there before the modern business class grew but these people – the rich people – bought into it and are as much responsible for it today as the authorities are. They are the ones – directly or indirectly – who the system runs on. They cannot change or get out of this system without losing all their business, parting from their comfortable relations with other wealthy families. It is too much change for them to imagine, and what is the alternative for them?

"They want change and reform – and they have asked for it in the past – but they also think that if they try to go to the streets to protest it will mean prison, the end of their businesses and their families being blacklisted."

Many people were withdrawing money from their banks and buying up gold and dollars in their fear, he said.

"And then we have another issue. The Assad family has long sided with Damascus, even though Aleppo is Syria's true industrial centre."

What could happen is a Tripoli-Benghazi situation whereby the business class in Aleppo turned against the regime and the capital stayed loyal, Samir continued. "So there are different possible outcomes when we talk about the wealthy people in Aleppo and Damascus. Anything is possible."

As we got closer to the area of Saboura, sixteen kilometres from Damascus, the road widened. It was after 9pm and pitch dark outside. Samir suddenly slowed down.

"This is bullshit," he says and I ask what's wrong. "Right now I'm afraid someone is going to jump out in front of us and either shoot at us or stop and take the car or something. This is no way to live."

"This is a wealthy area," I said, "no one is going to do anything here."

"I know, I'm not afraid of the people, but it's those who are saying there are armed gangs that are the ones who are actually putting them out on the streets in order to make people think there is a threat against the country," he said, exasperated. I asked him if he meant the government, and he nodded, focusing intently on the road ahead. "I shouldn't be feeling like this in my own country."

On the road it is obvious how much of an infrastructural difference existed between the capital and the towns and villages only a dozen or so kilometres out. Sewage seeped out onto the main streets, which were not even paved. Cheap locally-made motorbikes were omnipresent in the villages. These villagers were living hand to mouth, education ends at fifteen or eighteen when they are married off and begin another cycle of poverty. Healthcare is essentially non-existent. Syrian towns and villages are not like sub-Saharan Africa — there is electricity, water and television, though not always at the same time. But fifteen minutes down the road there were watches and earrings costing the equivalent of half a dozen homes in these villages. The Kia and Hyundai car revolution that now clogs the streets of Damascus, Aleppo and other cities was absent in these towns.

Samir's village was home to a member of the Syrian parliament who visited only a couple of times a year. At the gates of the main entrance to his villa stood two lion statues. The mansion had the best view in the village and its main door was adorned with a verse from the Quran in beautiful Arabic calligraphy. For all his influence and wealth he had only managed to erect two statues at either side of the entrance to the village in the past two years. He, like others in power, knew where to focus his attention, and it was not in Syria's rural towns and villages.

***

At First Cup, a popular restaurant in the Mezzah area of Damascus, I waited for Sami Moubayed to arrive to brief me on the mindset of the Damascenes. Sami was the editor-in-chief of *Forward* magazine, where I had once worked, and the author of several books on Syrian history in the twentieth century. He is widely regarded as the authority on the topic and on the country's leading figures. It was mid-May and, the day before, around forty-five protesters were reported to have been killed by the authorities during another wave of anti-regime protests that stretched from the villages around Deraa to Homs in the country's midlands and up to the Kurdish north east region.

He arrived in a rush and got straight to the point.

"In Aleppo I think there are several factors and not one alone. The overriding influence of the business community is a major factor and that applies to Damascus, too. Assad has been good to Aleppo since he came to power, the relationship with Turkey has become increasingly important and naturally it was his work that established a strong political relationship with Ankara that in turn created the foundation for business relationships between Aleppo and Turkish cities.

"As for Damascus there is a historical precedent," he continued, with his *argeleh* pipe in hand.

"The Damascus mindset, traditionally, has been this: 'Don't get us involved in the dirty work of revolution. We'll come up with a political solution, a prime minister and a government afterwards but we don't want anything to do with the strikes, the violence, and so forth.'" He went on to tell me how the Damascenes were dragged into revolt in the past.

"In 1925 Damascus went into revolt against the French and they suffered most, more than anyone else. Historically, during revolts the merchants and shops must close, said the protesters. The traditional rallying cry was '*sekkereh ya arasan, sekkereh*' which means 'close up you pimps, close up'.

"But what we need to ask ourselves now is this: Are we talking about the Damascus of 1925, or 1965 or of today? Today's Damascus has changed much over the decades and is now much less of the traditional city it was in the past. Numerically speaking it's not Damascus anymore – the majority of residents today are from the towns and villages around the capital. People who moved here a generation ago from Dariya, Madamiyeh, Douma, Deraa and other towns and villages, of course. Many living in the capital are from places where the uprising is taking place today."

"If this is the case then why isn't the capital burning up as the countryside is?" I asked.

"I think it's largely because of security reasons. The fear factor is a very strong one," he said. "The old families – let's divide them by rank and by generation – who are not as powerful as they used to be, I'm talking about my father's generation. They're not as politically in touch as they used to be. They would rather maintain the stability at this stage of their lives. They won't benefit from any real positive change and they are afraid for their families.

"The next generation, let's say, between thirty-five and fifty years old – they are Bashar al-Assad's generation. They have interests at stake. They have climbed the employment ladder to get where they are in private banks, in media companies and so on. There is a big portion of them who have become the modern Damascus over the last decade. They have young families so they don't want to rock the boat.

"And then you have the twenty- to thirty-five-year-olds. If they were to take to the streets they would make a real problem for the authorities. I think they are being held back by the influence of the older generations – the newly-weds and their own parents," he said.

"The Alawites, who are plenty in Damascus, wouldn't rise, nor would the Christians. There are 5 per cent who are very happy; they think they are in heaven on earth. There are 5 per cent who want a complete overhaul of the government and the authorities and then there is the silent majority, the silent 90 per cent. They couldn't care less; they want to go on with their daily lives. But, it must be said, if this 90 per cent cannot go on with their daily lives they may turn one way or another."

Sami asked me what I thought. I said that it seemed Damascenes didn't particularly care about what was happening to people in other parts of the country, that they only cared about their family and friends.

"There were problems when people in the Houran wanted to leave Syria, to join with Jordan during the last century," he told me. "Several members of the Damascene aristocracy said that they could 'go to hell for all we care' so this tells you something about how the elite in the capital thought about the countryside."

"So what do you think – are people thinking tribally?" I asked him.

"It breaks down to neighbourhood and clan. The Baath was founded on the poor people but it's the middle class that has most to lose now."

Were there no local leaders in Damascus putting their foot down and speaking out against what was happening around the country, and against the knock-on effect this was having on their businesses, I asked.

"You don't have local community organisations in Damascus. They have been completely vacuumed by the state. Look at the head of the Damascus chamber of commerce, he is an old and empty man, he has been put there, he wouldn't do or say anything that he is not told to do. The government is relying on him, on those like him to maintain the continuity of old. There are no business leaders of the calibre of old, those from before the Baath came to power."

Sami believed the absence of any independent leadership in the city actually worked against the government.

"I think there is now a major need of leadership qualities and this is in the interest of the street, the authorities and everyone else in Syria. There is a major void between the street and the state. There is no one that is well-regarded by the business class, the street and the authorities collectively."

The money in Damascus, Sami explained, was based on industry, cement and so on, as well as on banking, textiles, wool, and real estate centred both around the Old City and the city's suburban areas, such as Kafr Souseh, Mezzah and Yafour. "These businessmen [those in the Old City] don't spend money. They have one boy working for them on a very small wage; they sit in their shops drinking tea and *mette* [a tobacco drink] all day. They're sitting on fortunes in terms of property and goods. They don't retire; they go on working until they die.

"You can't predict what will happen. All of us analysts said a couple of months ago that Syria was last on the list of the countries to experience unrest."

I asked him about the situation with the country's Christians, the country's second most important minority and a community in a state of extreme fear during the unrest.

"Rural Christians are freaking out but I think the Damascene Christians are calm and taking the long view. It's amazing to see the difference between the urban and rural Christians. People like Colette Khoury [a novelist and poet], the urban wealthy Christians, are not afraid of a Salafist takeover, they have lived in peace with Muslims for decades, and their families before them have done so for much longer. In fact, the Christians would say that the land which today is called Syria has been theirs long before Islam ever appeared. I think the idea of an extremist Muslim takeover is ridiculous and has been sold by the regime," he said.

I put to him the hypothesis that if Aleppo was jealous of Damascus, a jealousy based on thousands of years of history, could we see Aleppo turning away from the regime in the way that Benghazi did in Libya?

"The people who protested in Aleppo [in April 2011] were students living in dorms on the campus of the university – they were not from Aleppo, they were from the countryside, from the Kurdish areas, the dustbowls around Hassake and Qamishli."

He put down his coffee and looked me straight in the eye.

"But if it happens in Aleppo, it will come to Damascus."

And it did. By February 2012 protests had taken place in numerous neighbourhoods around the capital.

"Anybody who was expecting the old quarters of the city to rise, like Amara, Qanawat, or Shaghour, is simply living on another planet," Sami told me as the revolt headed into its twelfth month. "These districts, once the hotbed for political dissent in the 1930s and 1940s, have more or less been emptied over the past thirty years, where most residents sold their property to wealthy Syrians wanting to live exotically, or investors who transformed them into boutique hotels and restaurants. The residents of these old quarters of Damascus then moved to the suburbs, to places like Madamiyeh, Harasta, Ghutta, and Qaboon. Let's keep in mind that fifty people on the streets of Damascus are more brave and courageous than 5,000 on the streets of Cairo, Sanaa, or Tunis."

***

Syrians have for decades been indoctrinated into the cult of the president. Throughout their schooling, they are taught to be in awe of and to love the president to the extent that thinking through and arguing the point of, for example, the timing and reason for the pro-Bashar demonstrations finds no logical answer. Many Syrians, who will argue and counterclaim over just about anything, have been dispassionate on the issue of the presidency. When discussing this specific issue, they have been trained not to think and never to argue.

Why were there pro-government demonstrations at the exact time when dozens were being gunned down in Syria's countryside? I myself witnessed the pro-government demonstration on 30 March that saw over 100,000 people clog the streets of Damascus. But, I would say 90 per cent of the people I saw were either school children, state employees, or the rough, young army conscripts who shouted about how they would "give our blood for you, oh Bashar". The Damascenes I know watched from their shop doors, from the balconies. They knew the government was carrying out murderous campaigns in the countryside. But they stayed silent.

Did they think: "I have my Kia Rio, I have my job in Syriatel, and I can holiday in Turkey a week in the year: I'm not worried about the uneducated masses in the countryside"? This certainly seems to have been the case.

II

THE MINORITIES AND SYRIA'S REVOLT

"There are no microbuses running today," I told a friend who had invited me to lunch at a restaurant high in the mountains close to the Syrian-Israeli demarcation border in south west Syria. I ended the call and waited ten more minutes before a microbus did, in fact, arrive and take me to Artouz where he was waiting to pick me up. The small town had seen several anti-government protests over the weeks of May and June but none had turned violent. The authorities would swiftly group together pro-government supporters and bus them to Artouz within a couple of hours of anti-government protesters having left. Syrian state television could then show that there was a demonstration; one in fulsome support of Bashar al-Assad. It was a convincing ploy that served to convince Syrians in other parts of the country that all was well for the president.

It was 1.15pm on 8 July — a Friday. Within fifteen minutes, millions of Syrians would flood out of mosques around the country. In Artouz, the authorities were ready. At the turnoff for the town of Qatana a mosque was being closely monitored. Several police cars were parked across the road. Thirty metres further up and out of sight of the mosque were three green buses. There was no one inside. On the pavement behind them were dozens of men armed with batons, helmets and shields. They lay in the shade counting down the minutes before the masses would flow from the mosque. They looked entirely, unnervingly, non-plussed.

My friend picked me up in a silver Kia almost directly in front of the security officers and we passed on to Qatana looking straight ahead through the windscreen. By the time we arrived, it was 1:28pm according to the car clock. By now, small numbers had started leaving the two main mosques in the centre of the town. We took a detour to pick up some friends before heading on to Erneh, a village under the shadow of Sheikh Mountain. The only road to Erneh passed close to the town's main mosque. Our deviated route added a few minutes to our journey but saw us alight at the street where one of the chief mosques stood. I looked back in the direction of the mosque to see a scene I had expected, but still found hard to believe: a crowd of perhaps 1,000 people jammed together, jumping up and down. They were screaming for freedom. Women poured water over the crowd as the sun beat down in forty degree heat.

Qatana is a religiously-diverse army town twenty-eight kilometres south west of Damascus. It has a population of about 30,000 and is about 65 per cent Sunni, 20 per cent Christian and 15 per cent Alawite. The latter moved to the town when it was established as an army base during hostilities with Israel in the 1970s. Historically the town is not an Alawite stronghold. Alawite families are viewed as outsiders today, something that has added to the sectarian tension there.

As we drove out of the town, another group of about a hundred men carrying Syrian flags marched silently – but with gusto, and without any hint of fear in their bulging eyes – past our car from a mosque to meet those inside the town. There was no sign of any military presence.

We left Qatana's heaving protesters behind us, but when we reached our destination among the acres of cherry, apple and almond trees and a stone's throw from the Syrian-Israeli demilitarised zone, another newly-politicised group from the spectrum of Syria's religious make-up awaited.

Erneh is a Druze stronghold. One must pass through a checkpoint to get there at which you will be turned back if you are not known. My friend was recognised as he had been involved in rebuilding a church in the nearby village of Qalaa the previous year.

Wissam's Paradise, a restaurant surrounded by shady springs, draws an almost exclusively Christian clientele, and has done for years. In the summer of 2010, a few Muslim families would come for lunch and take in the fresh air, but there were none that July. Local Alawites make up the remainder the patrons.

My friend and I spoke to an Alawite police officer who evidently didn't realise I was a foreign journalist. He said the police and security were waiting for the protests to turn violent in Qatana. "When they turn to violence against government or police buildings, the army and security forces will deal with the problem." He said this meant shooting at the protesters.

Over the course of the afternoon, we ate hummus, salad and barbecued chicken interspersed with shots of *arak*. People danced *dabke* – a traditional fast-paced dance where participants hold hands and move in circles. At one point a group of young men began chanting "Abu Hafez" in reference to Bashar al-Assad, whose oldest son is named Hafez. Those who didn't chant looked on, clapping their hands. Some cast careful stares towards those (including me) who didn't partake in this spontaneous pro-regime showing.

That day fifteen people were reported killed in anti-government protests across the country. In Hama almost half a million people took to the streets to demand an end to the regime – the largest number reached in a year of protest.

With the thousand-strong crowd calling for the end of the regime and their fellow townspeople, the Christians, chanting their undying support for Bashar al-Assad, that Friday afternoon served as a timely reminder of the delicate balance in Qatana. More critically, such divisions and tensions between religious groups were being replicated in towns and cities right around Syria.

Christians laid claim to the territories of today's Syria long before Muslim armies surged up from the Arabian peninsula and reached Damascus in the middle of the seventh century.

The largest Christian denomination is Greek Orthodox with Syriac Catholic, Syriac Orthodox, and small Maronite and Protestant communities present right around the country. Intermarriage between different rites is customary, though frequently regarded as less than ideal.

Syrian Christians deal with civil issues like marriage, divorce and inheritance through their own laws. Though it happens, Syrian Christians do not accept marriage with Muslims. Conversely, Syria's Muslims have little problem accepting a Christian in marriage so long as he or she converts to Islam. I've heard regular accounts of how young Christian/Muslim couples run away to Lebanon to be married in secret in an act called *khatifah*.

The vast majority, however, belong to the Eastern rite, which has existed in Syria since the earliest days of Christianity. They view themselves as very different from western Christians and especially exceptional with regard to their fellow non-Christian countrymen.

Syria's rural Christians lived in a state of denial during the unrest. Anyone who questioned the actions of the regime was castigated: a family I know that saw their son detained for over a month by the *mukhabarat*, after being framed by a jealous colleague at a factory for stealing, nonetheless remained behind the regime during Syria's revolt.

Like other minorities, Christians, from Deraa in the south to Aleppo to Qamishli in the north east, were very afraid. Christians have disowned elements of their communities that have displayed anti-regime rhetoric. One woman relayed to me how her cousins who were members of the outlawed Communist party were then shunned from the family. George Sabra, a well-known Christian activist and a leading member of the opposition group, the Syrian National Council, was cursed by Qatana's Christian population for his opposition to the government.

In the Christian neighbourhoods of Damascus and Aleppo, where apartments regularly fetch 20 million Syrian pounds (US$400,000) while nearby non-Christian flats sell for less than a quarter of that, people refused to believe the truth. Everything was fine. The trouble in the countryside was caused by only a few Salafist gangs brought here by the Saudis, they said. The regime was strong. On countless occasions I was told "it will be over soon".

There had been nightly anti-government protests in Qatana for over a month in May and June. On 27 May, three protesters were killed by security forces, which resulted in the protests growing in size and frequency. One Christian man was reported to have been stabbed for displaying a photo of the president on his car in mid-June. Then, in early July, Sunni and Alawite youths hurled stones at each other on a main street next to a security building.

At a dinner party among friends one evening in June, two Christian families celebrated the marriage of relatives. However, the topic of conversation swiftly turned to what was known in common conversation as 'The Situation'.

"Al Jazeera can go to hell. I've stopped watching it completely," one man said.

"There are people coming in from fifteen villages tomorrow [Friday] to protest, I hope they get what they deserve," said another.

The same man questioned what happened to thirteen-year-old Hamza al-Kateeb, who was reportedly tortured by security forces for attending an anti-government demonstration with his father close to Deraa in Syria's south. "Al Jazeera is spreading lies," he said. "They killed him but he wasn't tortured like they are saying."

"The president has been very good to Christians," added one woman at the gathering. "We don't want change, we are happy."

"Saudi Arabia is behind these troubles. Recently a butcher was paid 30,000 lira [US$620] to shoot at demonstrators," said one man in his fifties who invited me in for coffee upon seeing me on the street in Qatana the following afternoon, as protesters marched 500 metres from us.

"Bandar Bin Sultan has long been friends with America," he added, referring to the Saudi prince who, state media outlets claimed, was attempting to sow unrest in Syria.

Protests had taken place in May but were small and disorganised, said other locals. The cause of the demonstrations in Qatana, it was said by one local woman, was an incident involving a Sunni man who mocked a passing vehicle containing soldiers. One soldier threw a stone at the man, who was severely injured by the blow. His family threatened to take revenge against the soldiers – said to have been mostly Alawite – if the man died from his injuries.

A week later protesters marched on a building belonging to security services and were shot at.

"We could hear the shots from our balcony," another Christian man, a school teacher, told me at the time.

The following day, authorities allowed the families of those killed to bury their dead. The same evening a pro-government rally was granted 'permission' to take place in the town.

I participated in and listened to countless conversations with Christians in Syria during the 2011 uprising. Some asked what the protesters would do if they got what they were calling for – the downfall of the Assad regime. Others said they should all be shot. Almost all feared an Islamic takeover.

The Christians I knew owned cars, and were employed as doctors, dentists, by the various government ministries and are well-regarded in many circles. Christians, arguably the wealthiest minority in the country (more so than Alawites even), occupied many positions of authority within the regime. Colette Khoury, for instance, served as culture adviser to President Assad and wrote for a state-owned newspaper. The regime sought good relations with Christians and, although a Christian cannot become president, they were taken care of by the regime.

In April 2011 rumours of sectarian targeting spread like wildfire among the Damascus Christian population. In the Abbasiyeen area of the city, men in cars were apparently firing gunshots into the air. A twenty-five-year-old girl who worked at a pharmaceutical company told me how three churches in her area had received letters saying "you're next". It was interpreted as being a message from the Islamist protesters, meaning that once they got Bashar al-Assad out, Syria's Christians would be the next to go.

***

Syria's Kurds largely reside in the north eastern region of the country, including the cities and towns of Qamishli, Raqqa, Hassake and the large swathes of rural hinterlands around these cities. Kurds, who are predominantly Sunni, are the largest ethnic minority in Syria, accounting for around 10 per cent of the population.

In 1920 the Treaty of Sèvres, which created modern day Iraq and Syria, included the creation of an independent Kurdish state. However, with the overthrow of the Ottoman monarchy by Kemal Atatürk and the negotiation of the Treaty of Lausanne in 1923, the idea of a Kurdish state was dropped. Under the French mandate over Syria, Syrian Kurds enjoyed certain privileges. Their admission to military and administrative positions was facilitated, for instance.

When the Baath (Renaissance) party took control of Syria in 1963, followed by an internal military coup led by Hafez al-Assad in 1970, Arab nationalist sentiment was elevated to the extent that Kurds were sidelined. In 1962, an 'exceptional census' stripped some 120,000 Kurds of their Syrian citizenship. They became unable to apply for a passport, register their children to attend school or have marriages registered.

According to Jordi Tejel's book, *Syria's Kurds: History, Politics, and Society* (Routledge, 2009), an alliance established by Hafez al-Assad in the 1970s broke down in 2004 when an uprising followed a football game in the remnants of the Damascus Spring of 2000–01, the 2004 Kurdish revolt serving to embolden the Kurds in their push for autonomy and respect.

Syria and Turkey nearly went to war in the 1990s when Damascus was accused of sheltering Abdullah Öcalan, the leader of the Kurdistan Workers' Party (PKK).

In the winter of 2009, I visited south east Turkey and Iraqi Kurdistan. My return journey back to Damascus took me over the border through Qamishli (this border is not open to vehicle traffic, and I witnessed the remarkable sight of hundreds of people walking back into Syria with pots, pans and other household items bought in Turkey). By chance, and probably illegally, I took an army bus back down to Damascus. The soldiers, conscripted for the two-year military duty, were all Kurdish, young and of minimal education. They told me they received 500SYP (about US$10) per month. They were returning to Damascus to their military bases, following a break at home with their families which they were allowed once every few months. Two years later, in the midst of the 2011 uprising, I wondered what was asked of these illiterate and destitute boys in their defence of 'Syria'.

But Kurds, though certainly somewhat isolated, at least fall into the broader Sunni class – the majority. Their qualms about the regime fit well with those of the thousands of other Sunni Syrians who filled the streets of dozens of towns and cities each and every Friday during the uprising.

In late May and into June, protests against the Syrian government took place in a plethora of Kurdish districts. In the streets they held up banners with the Kurdish word *azadi* (*hurriyi* in Arabic), or freedom. They had felt the long arm and iron fist of the Assad government for decades but now they were not alone.

As protests spread in April, a decree was announced by President Assad stating that an estimated 300,000 Kurds who had been declared stateless in the 1962 census were to be granted citizenship in one of several concessions to protesters at the time. The speed with which Assad acted to change the law shows that it was not a case of inability to grant these people citizenship, but of a lack of desire.

But the Kurds of Syria were by no means the central kernel of resistance to the regime during the 2011 uprising. They were very much on the fringe. The government did not send the army or security services into Kurdish towns. Why not? The answer, addressed elsewhere in this book, is tied in with capabilities and the regime's tactics in suppressing protests.

The Syrian authorities had not restrained themselves from acting in the past. In March 2004, Syrian security forces intervened in a clash between supporters of rival Kurdish and Arab football teams in Qamishli, leaving several dead and many injured. According to The Society for Threatened Peoples, in the demonstrations which followed this incident, "at least thirty Kurdish civilians were killed, over a 1,000 were injured and more than 2,500 were arrested. At least five Kurds were tortured to death during imprisonment following the demonstrations. Six Kurds were murdered during their military service."

The same report stated that, in May 2005, "Sheikh Maschuk (Maashuq) Al Khaznawi, a popular Kurdish religious leader, and outspoken critic of the Ba'ath regime, was murdered, having 'disappeared' a few weeks previously. Although Syrian authorities claimed the Sheikh was murdered by bandits, his family said Al Khaznawi's body bore marks of severe torture and that he was treated in Tesrin hospital for fifteen hours before he died on 30 May.

"The Sheikh's death caused a huge outpouring of grief among Kurds and demonstrations took place in Qamishli. Once again, Syrian security forces intervened and opened fire on the crowd. More than fifty Kurds were arrested." [sic]

Mohammad (who asked for his real name not to be published), a twenty-three-year-old Kurdish man, met me at the President's Bridge in central Damascus. It was 18 July and over fifty people had been killed across the country during the previous weekend.

He was thin and slightly bent over. He began in Arabic but we switched to English when the conversation turned to 'The Situation' in order to be more covert. We went to an up-market café close by, but Mohammad surveyed his surroundings uneasily. When I broached the topic of Syria's unrest, he insisted we went elsewhere to talk. I explained that we were safe; there were a lot of people around us but none within earshot. His hands were tough and cut in places. He had finished his final English literature university exams three weeks previously and begun working in construction thereafter. He told me he earned 600SYP (or US$12) per day working from 8am to 5pm, six days a week. His story is repeated thousands of times across Syria.

Mohammad, one of thirteen children from a village close to Qamishli in Syria's north east Kurdish heartland, lived with three of his brothers in the largely Kurdish Wadi Bashara suburb close to Dummar. In softly spoken words he told me of his dislike of the Assad regime. "When Nasser [Gamal Abdul Nasser, the former president of Egypt] took control of Syria he wanted to move all the Kurds out of the north east of Syria and put them along the border with Iraq further south. The Syrian authorities let them do so, in theory, [but] fortunately for us, the war with Israel started a couple of years later and they didn't get the chance.

"You have heard of the saying that your enemy's enemy is your friend – many Kurds like Israel." This was a startling statement to hear from a Syrian and illustrated the depth of extreme dislike for the regime held by Kurds.

The Kurds of Syria vary, he continued; some are conservative and some less so. "But we all want the regime to go. They have been horrible for us." However, like those I interviewed from other minorities, he would not sacrifice the end of the Assad rule for a more strict Islamist authority.

There were limits, he said, to what being part of the larger majority brings: "Yes we are Sunni, but the thing you are missing is that Syria's Sunnis are mostly Arab. We are not Arab. The name of this country is the Syrian Arab Republic so in name, this is not our country. We are not represented and that is how the regime thinks about the Kurds."

What was striking about Mohammad is that he seemed to still be living in January 2011. He talked in hushed tones, when the entire city around him was speaking freely about 'The Situation'. At this time the authorities had much more to worry about than simple rambling speech and opinion – people were gathering in large and threatening numbers. He was not excited about the incredible changes taking place at the time and those which appeared on the horizon with the Assad regime beginning to crumble. Bitterness seemed to have paralysed hope – what the Kurds have had to endure at the hands of the Assad regime runs so deep that even revolution does not appeal to their interests.

But maybe this tells us something else. The repression and cruelty experienced by the Syrian Kurds for so long have not been, or cannot have been, washed away during a few months of unrest that may or very well may not succeed in overthrowing the regime.

This may indicate a sense of hopelessness amongst Kurds, even in the event that the protestors succeed. They are, after all, according to Mohammad, non-Arabs chased out of Turkey over the past one hundred years and, as such, homeless.

He said that although Kurds had been the number one thorn in the side of the government in Damascus for decades, and though Kurds were normally the first to rebel given half a chance, anti-regime protests have been notably quiet in the Kurdish regions.

"That is because we don't feel that this uprising is ours. We have tried for decades and have gotten nowhere. So now when it seems like something may change, it looks like we are being left behind," said Mohammad. "This is an Arab uprising and we are not Arab," he repeated.

Many Kurds had made their way to Damascus in search of work in any sector they could find over the past couple of decades, for lack of opportunities in their home cities. The men who sell cigarettes, old books, pots and pans on and under the President's Bridge and elsewhere, those who work in kiosks and those who light and manage the *argelehs* in the city's hundreds of restaurants, are almost all Kurdish. They work in construction and have built illegal houses without electricity, water or sewage systems. In the microbuses they speak Kurdish on their mobile phones as Arabic-speaking passengers look on.

They are Syria's third class citizens. Even the Iraqi refugees who have poured over the border since 2003 and who continue to compete with Syrians for jobs are better treated and respected than the Kurds. The teaching of their language is forbidden. They cannot build private schools like, for example, Christians can.

Many dream of having a stable job. One thirty-something man from Qamishli who worked in the Ministry of Social Affairs and Labour told me, amazingly, that in twenty-seven years his monthly salary would increase from US$200 to US$300. I laughed out loud when he told me. I thought he was joking. He was not.

Syria's Kurds are unequalled in their mistreatment by the Assad government. But within the realm of the 2011 uprising, they were, by July, the odd man out. They are a minority that has suffered much under both Assad regimes and been rejected by the wider Arab population. Nevertheless, largely Sunni, they share a significant identity with the anti-regime protestors even if, like other minorities, they are terrified of an Islamist oriented government. They are caught between two stools.

***

For centuries prior to the rule of the Assads, the Alawites constituted Syria's most repressed and exploited minority. Most were servants, or tenant farmers or labourers working for Sunni land-owners along the country's coastal mountain region.

When France occupied Syria it organised an Alawite sub-state that ran from Syria's coastal border with Turkey in the north, down the coast to the border with Lebanon.

Many Alawites I know drink and frequent nightclubs regularly. They don't go to mosques to pray. They hang out with foreigners. They don't fast during Ramadan.

Yet Lattakia, an Alawite stronghold on the north Syria coast, but with large Christian and Sunni populations, was one of the first cities to join in anti-government protests in March and April of 2011.

Government-backed Alawite gangs called *shabiha* (the violent, mostly Alawite gangs that brutally enforced the regime's will) reportedly roamed the streets of Lattakia and Banias shooting into shops and houses in an effort to drive fear back into the hearts of the residents there. In early July, a Christian doctor told me the Alawite families living in the centre of Qatana, which is predominately Sunni and was the heart of the anti-government protest movement in the town, had all left out of fear of the protesters.

On 17 July, I met Abed and Ali, two Alawite friends from the coastal cities of Tartous and Lattakia. The day before, a Saturday, more than thirty people had been killed, mostly on the streets of Homs.

We arranged to meet at a restaurant called First Cup in Mezzah, but they changed the venue at the last minute as it was apparently known as a *shabiha* and pro-government restaurant. We instead decided on a café close by where menus are presented on an iPad.

Abed worked at an embassy in the capital, Ali in the country's public sector. They were both twenty-eight years old.

Ali first told me his car was broken into by a taxi driver outside the faculty of literature in Mezzah on a recent afternoon in full view of university guards. Petty crime was growing in the city as the government's grip on security unravelled.

I didn't know Ali, the man I made contact with, very well and he asked me to give them my opinion. He was clearly nervous to begin talking about such a sensitive topic. The embassy worker, whom I had not met before, seemed much calmer. I told them that the government was doing terrible things but that the alternative at that time might be worse. I said I was interviewing people from different religious sects to try to understand what they thought, showing them my journalist accreditation card and hoping to look legitimate.

Within a month of the unrest beginning Abed's parents went back to their village in Tartous. "They teach Arabic and because there are no foreign students in Damascus any more they went back home, but there was another reason for them to leave." Abed added how his father had been insulted in shops and when he dealt with people in public as people suspected he was Alawite "because of his accent". Syrians' accents vary from region to region but the coastal accent is typically associated with Alawite authority in Syria. He wanted to see the end of the regime; he no longer spoke to his brother because of their differing political views.

Ali said that he was behind the president and that the protesters were essentially stupid.

"I don't understand why they are protesting. They are calling for the fall of the regime but what will they do then? I know the government has done things that were not right. I don't want to say I am with the government or against the protesters. I'm somewhere in the middle," he said.

I told him that I assumed all Alawites were 100 hundred per cent behind the regime.

"Not at all," they both exclaimed simultaneously.

"Many Alawites are against the regime. Aref Dalila [a leading opposition figure] is Alawite and from Lattakia, the Alawites have been mistreated by the regime too. I know someone who is very close to the president. Bashar says that if he has to, he will step down as president. But he won't leave when the country is facing such turmoil," said Ali.

"The regime needs to do three things: it needs to change the media laws, it needs to hold free elections and it needs to wipe out Article 8 of the constitution [which says the leading party in Syria is the Baath party]."

But he asked me how the Sunni farmers in Deraa got their hands on weapons. "They have satellite phones. They are poor farmers – how could they afford these phones, where did they come from?" he queried, implying that outside elements smuggled them over the Jordanian border.

Abed disagreed.

"They [the regime] have had four months; they said they have ended the state of emergency [which allows the government to detain Syrians without a warrant issued from a court or judge]. They have had time but they are not doing anything – they can't do anything."

Ali argued that the people in Hama, which for a time in July became a *de facto* free city, and where almost half a million anti-regime protesters gathered each Friday, were "very conservative".

"When [American] Ambassador Robert Ford went to Hama there were reports that he gave the protesters satellite phones and other things. No one knows exactly what happened but why not send the Indian ambassador – someone who is unbiased?"

Abed thought that the idea to send Ford to Hama on 7 July was agreed to by the American and Syrian governments well in advance, as it suited the interests of both. The visit was followed by a break-in by pro-government supporters at the American embassy in Damascus. "I think they all agreed to this. For the American government they can show the world that they care about the Syrian protesters and are trying to do something. For the Syrian government it suits them because it takes attention away from the issue of protests and they can use America's interference to drum up more support among Syrians. They can now say that the Americans are working to destabilise Syria. It's really quite simple."

Every time a waiter or customer came close, the two men broke off in mid-sentence and turned silent.

Ali thought they were receiving arms from outside: "Khaddam [Abdul Halim Khaddam was a former vice-president and, after criticising Bashar al-Assad in 2005, was sent into exile] said on television that he was sending arms to the protesters and he would continue to do so for as long as he could – what more proof do you want?"

The problem, believed Ali, is that the protesters were uneducated and poor people: "They don't really know what they want. The government is saying 600 security personnel and soldiers have been killed by gangs. OK, let's presume they are exaggerating and [it is] half that number. This makes 300 but this is still a lot."

I told him I saw students beaten and arrested for calling, peacefully, for freedom two weeks previously in Baramkeh, Damascus.

"Like the president said in his last speech – the security services don't know how to deal with such things when they happen. They are not educated and reasonable people."

We ran out of time on that occasion, but agreed to meet again in a couple of days, which we did at a café in Dummar outside the capital that was supposed to be full of infiltrators – the anti-regime people, joked Ali.

He told me how the government was starting to employ people in the public sector who could not read and write in a bid to pacify the masses. Surely, I argued, this was not the solution. He agreed.

He then pointed out that two days previously a taxi driver had been fined for smoking while driving.

"He said, 'it will take me ten days to get the 2,000 back so if someone comes and says they will pay me to go and protest against the government I will do it'."

Abed arrived shortly after and said he felt humiliated after watching a video of almost-naked men being abused and beaten on BBC Arabic. He could not believe his countrymen were doing such things. Friends, but adversaries in discussions on Syrian politics, Ali and Abed glanced at each other. Ali said the *shabiha* gangs are in all likelihood unpaid. "They come from the mountains around Lattakia and the coast and they carry out such things because of their alliances with people in the security apparatus. They don't attack people for money; they do it for favours, for power." Ali said they were not to be messed with.

"There must be such a massive propaganda machine inside the army for them to do such things. The soldiers had to be told that they are shooting Islamists, or that the people protesting are not Syrian. The rallying cry of many protests is *Allah u Akhbar* [god is greatest] and when the soldiers hear this, they, who are largely uneducated, must think they are Salafists or something," said Abed.

"The president must see what is happening on Al Jazeera or on YouTube," added Abed, "but he is powerless. I think the important person in this situation is Maher [Bashar's younger brother and *de facto* head of the Syrian army] – he has the power to rein in the security officers and the circle around Bashar who are filling his head with propaganda."

Abed thought that the protestors should continue to take to the streets until "we see elections laws implemented. Only then should the regime be given a chance."

Ali disagreed: "We need to give the government a chance and the people demonstrating have to take a step back. Civil war is becoming more and more real every day now." It gave me hope for open democracy to see such views expressed between friends. Maybe they were being polite for my sake.

***

During the unrest the Syrian government launched a campaign to show how much the state has taken care of the country's minorities.

Good relations with the Christian community were most visible through numerous interviews with leading church representatives on the state television channel and on Dunia TV, a ferocious supporter of the regime and majority-owned by Rami Makhlouf, the president's cousin.

The latter would broadcast interviews with local priests and Shia sheikhs, carefully choreographed on the calm banks of the Euphrates in Syria's eastern desert region. Sometimes they prayed together on air, especially at Christmas.

By doing so, the regime sought to draw in supporters from the country's minorities. If priests and Shia sheikhs appeared on television saying they fully supported the president then their followers would feel obliged – in this most religious of countries – to follow suit.

Are Syria's Shia community supportive of the regime because they are a minority or because of the links to Alawite Islam, an offshoot of the former?

To try and find out, I spoke to an old friend I hadn't seen in over a year.

Mazen was a former bodybuilder. Standing at six foot four inches he appeared every inch the tough man. But he was not. He owned a confectionary shop in the Christian area of Bab Touma in Damascus.

Around the capital the traditional Shia neighbourhoods are to be found in Saida Zainab in the south east, and parts of the Old City.

One alleyway off Bab Touma square informs you exactly who lives here. A huge poster of Hassan Nasrallah, the leader of Hezbollah, tells you this is Shia country.

I met Ali in Bab Touma on 12 July. At the adjacent square a sound engineer was testing the stage's speaker system in preparation for yet another pro-Assad rally. On the streets around, peddlers sell Syrian and Hezbollah flags of varying sizes and pictures of *ma'limna* (our boss – Bashar). Mazen was in front of me, giving a young man a hard time about something at the top of Bab Touma square. He saw me but I gave them a few minutes to sort out whatever it was they were talking about.

We walked to a restaurant owned by his friend. Mazen is from this general locality.

He had recently returned from a trip to Denmark and told me that everyone there had the wrong opinion of Syria.

"What happened in Egypt has a lot of consequences for Syria. America has lost its number one friend in the region. Mubarak is gone and Washington can't depend on the new Egyptian government for anything right now. So they have lost Egypt and are looking for a new country. They want Syria because it borders Israel and they want to use our country as a buffer."

I asked him why America would need Syria if it had Iraq.

"Believe me, America does not have Iraq. If anyone has Iraq it's the Iranians."

We moved on to talk about Hama, where media reports said 500,000 people demonstrated on the previous two Fridays.

"People in Hama are tough, they are hard-headed," said Mazen.

I asked why.

"You know what happened in 1982."

"Yes, Hafez al-Assad killed over 10,000 people there," I said.

"Right, but because of this European tourists love Syria. If he didn't wipe out the Muslim Brotherhood then, Syria would not be the country it was for the past thirty years. If the Muslim Brotherhood got stronger and somehow got control or formed a coup, we would have a very different Syria; foreigners would not have been able to enjoy our history and culture. There would have been no Arabic students. The whole world would have had a much bigger problem with Syria.

"And what was the American ambassador doing in Hama last week? He went all the way up there just to have a look around?" Mazen was quite animated now. "Of course he didn't – he went there to meet someone. Why not send the Indian or Brazilian or Korean ambassador to Hama?"

It was almost forty degrees outside and the restaurant, at 6.30 in the evening, was practically empty.

"My mother is seventy-two now but she tells me that when she was small she walked with her father in Qamarieh street [a main throughway in the Old City] and people would throw things at her and her father because they were Shia."

I asked Mazen who did this, were they Christians?

"No, they were Sunni, and this division, this way of thinking still exists today."

"So am I right to say that Shia people in Syria are supporting the regime because it is Alawite?" I replied.

"There are some historical similarities between Shias and Alawites but in reality, today, they are like this." Mazen held up his two hands in opposite directions. "They drink and go to nightclubs. Shia don't."

I ask Mazen what his family and friends thought about the unrest in Syria, if they were with or against the government.

"My family think the same as me, more or less. They support the president and want the government to stay. Of course, we need so many changes in this country. As for my friends, we don't really talk about politics." I asked why. "Listen, people in the Middle East can't have differing opinions like you do in Denmark or England or wherever. There you can talk and argue on television or anywhere for an hour and when you're done you can shake hands and be friends, there are no issues. But here, if people have an argument about something they will leave from different doors."

Mazen told me he thought it was outsiders who were responsible for the trouble in Syria. "There is definitely something from them [Israel and America]. I don't know exactly what it is, but they are trying to do something."

He said that he had he read in an Israeli newspaper via the internet recently that Germany was offering 70,000 passports to Israelis to return to Germany because they were afraid of an upcoming regional war in the Middle East. He had also read somewhere that Iran had told western governments that if Turkey was ever used as a base to bomb Syria, Tehran would shoot them out of the sky.

"Turkey is in a difficult position because they are trying to enter the EU, but they want to have some control of the Middle East at the same time," he stated.

"They are trying to break up Hezbollah, Iran and Syria. America is trying to get into Syria but they can't – Syria has too many cards to play. We have [at that time] Hamas, we have Hezbollah, we have Iran, and Turkey is also becoming important. The West has very few options with Syria."

The day before I met Mazen, on 11 July, pro-government mobs attacked the American and French embassies in Damascus. A Syrian flag was raised in place of the American one and guards defending the French embassy had to fire live ammunition in the air to keep a rampaging mob armed with a battering ram out.

As we got up to leave, Mazen looked over at his friend, the owner of the restaurant. He was speaking in fluent German to a couple of foreigners about, I think, how he was going to decorate the walls of his restaurant. Mazen turned to me. "The president needs to, and can, do something to bring all the people of Syria together again. It is very simple, I think." I ask him what that was.

"A war with Israel. If he started a war the entire country, Christian, Sunni, Alawite, Shia and all the rest would unite around him. What's going on now [the uprising] would be forgotten, we would be united again. More importantly, Stephen, war with Israel is what everyone wants, and this would be a war that includes Hezbollah, Iran, America ... everyone." His eyes were alight.

***

The Druze are a tenth century offshoot of Ismaili Islam and emerged and briefly proselytised in what is modern Syria. Their religion incorporates many beliefs from a range of monotheistic and other religions. The Druze religion is a closed one – individuals cannot enter or leave it. According to Minority Rights Group International, the first Druze settlers probably arrived in the Jabal Druze from Mount Lebanon and Aleppo at the end of the seventeenth century, and today their numbers in Syria are around 700,000: "Their chief concerns were to establish communities where they would not be molested by Ottoman authorities or the Sunni population, and that were defensible against Bedouin raids. As a result of the events of 1860 in Mount Lebanon, the Jabal experienced a massive influx of Druze migrants from Lebanon. Throughout the nineteenth century the Ottomans unsuccessfully attempted to subdue the Druze into submission to taxation and conscription like the rest of the province of Syria." About 15,000 Druze have lived under Israeli military occupation on the Golan since 1967 and reports indicate that they were fervently pro-Assad during the unrest.

The Druze of Erneh and surrounding villages in south west Syria are a secretive community. Their women wear a white shawl over their heads, the older men do likewise. They work on tiny farms in mountain-side hamlets harvesting cherries, apples and olives, driving small tractors at speed up and down the sun-kissed hillsides. They sell cherry juice to the Christians who arrive in Erneh each Friday to escape the heat and to dine at local open-air restaurants.

The Druze build temples on almost impassable mountain sides in order to prove their faith. Their temples are usually Spartan one-roomed houses lit by a red light.

These Druze communities shy from outside interest – even from local Syrians, who regard them as peaceful. "Leave them alone, don't touch their land and they are fine," a Christian who lived close to Erneh told me.

However, the Druze homeland is based in the Houran and Jabal Druze regions in south Syria, areas strongly associated with revolt in Syria's modern history

Were Druze people involved in the uprising in Deraa and other local villages?

Michael Provence, the author of *The Great Syrian Revolt and the Rise of Arab Nationalism* (University of Texas Press, 2005) and an expert on the Syrian Druze, says perhaps, but not on sectarian grounds.

"I think there is plenty of Druze support for the protests. As a small, historically significant, and committed Arabist minority, we will not see 'Druze protest', but there are protesters who are Druze, if you see the difference. There have certainly been protests in majority Druze towns and villages," he wrote via email in July 2011.

"The government has not worried enough about these protests to crush them violently. The government considers 'Muslim' protest an existential threat. There is no worry about any existential threat from any other Syrian minority group. There was at least one, and probably several, marches in Suweida, at least one led by lawyers," he says, recounting that he knows personally a number of Druze activists who have been "critical and courageously opposed to the government for years".

"For pious Sunnis, the situation is different. They can, and often appear to be, opposing the government as 'Muslims'. As members of the majority religion, opposing a regime they define as Alawite, this is understandable. Even if protestors are secular, the government has attempted to condemn protesters as Salafist criminals. Obviously the government cannot justify repressing secular, multi-sectarian, Arab nationalist patriots."

There have been, for decades, countless numbers of sectarian attacks in which the regime has either been complicit or simply turned a blind eye. On 30 October 2004, two Assyrian Christians were reportedly murdered by an off-duty Sunni military officer and his brother in Hassake province. The Syrian authorities responded to the resulting protests from the Assyrian community by arresting twelve Assyrians. No charges were brought against the perpetrators of the murders.

In one amusing case in 2010, an institute in the Christian town of Maaloula teaching the Aramaic language, the language spoken by Jesus Christ, was closed down by the authorities because it was said to resemble Hebrew too much. A government official later said authorities were trying to rectify the situation. It is mishandling like this that has proved to push the population away from the state. Simple incompetence, in this proud society, can translate into much more severe consequences down the road.

***

Back in Qatana, the town twenty-eight kilometres south west of the capital, a microcosm of the delicate balances of sects and religions in Syria, the first signs of the uprising, which in late July was over four months old, took on a sectarian tone.

Running gun battles between state security forces and Alawite youths and, on the other side, Sunni Muslims became a daily occurrence for over a week in that month, illustrating a growing split among the town's population as anti-regime protests grew in frequency and size.

Qatana's Christians, who account for twenty per cent of the local population and are largely located in the northern neighbourhoods of the town, were terrified at the time.

"Early this morning there was automatic gun fire for over a minute next to our house," a resident told me on 16 July. "It started on Wednesday night when there was shooting between the security and Sunni Muslims. They cut the electricity and phone lines for several hours. We were in total fear."

Qatana is home to Maher al-Assad's feared 4th division, which is said to have been responsible for some of the most violent crackdowns on anti-regime protesters around Syria. Maher, Bashar's excessively violent younger brother, is the actual head of the Syrian army and directly commands the Presidential Guard which oversees security for Damascus. It was he, it is said, who put an end to Bashar's talk of political reform in 2000. It was also Maher's 4th Division which attempted to violently crush protests in Deraa in the early days of the revolt.

By then, as Ramadan appeared on the horizon (which meant millions of Syrians attending prayers every evening), the possibility of sectarian bloodletting, based on allegiance and opposition to the Alawite-dominated regime, became a growing possibility. Many minorities feared a repeat of the violence that saw neighbouring Iraq and Lebanon drawn into sectarian conflict and civil war. Should the regime fall, they fear the rise of the Muslim Brotherhood, which was savagely repressed by Hafez al-Assad in Hama in 1982.

On 3 February 1982, word of an uprising in Hama was announced by leading members of the Muslim Brotherhood. Through mosque loudspeakers the Brotherhood called for jihad against government targets, including leading Baathists and military complexes in the city. Dozens of government officials were killed and several military bases were overrun by the Brotherhood by daylight.

The Assad regime, headed by Bashar's uncle and commanding general of the army, Rifaat al-Assad, then employed 12,000 troops as well as military aircraft and shells to quell the revolt. Between 10,000 and 30,000 people were killed in the following three weeks. The Islamic revolt was destroyed.

In addition to emphasising the point that an overwhelming majority of Syrians are 'united', the regime has obliquely used the threat of Islamic fundamentalism to draw the country's minorities to its side by repeatedly claiming during the unrest that armed Islamist gangs were responsible for all the deaths of civilians and hundreds of army and security personnel.

Many Alawite and Christian families fled Qatana in mid-July because of the fear of sectarian targeting as the protest movement grew. Shops, businesses and cars in the town were set alight and graffiti was sprayed on Christian businesses again, saying 'you're next'. The extended family of a Christian woman from Qatana fled to the town where I lived – eight kilometres away – as it was believed she was hiding three anti-regime protesters and they were afraid of being implicated in her actions. The unrest was quite literally tearing families apart.

A woman from the town said that on 15 July, the day before the army entered and sealed off Qatana, some of the Druze community, who live in villages in the mountains north west of Qatana, were stopped at military checkpoints. "They want to fight the Muslims and to protect the Alawites and Christians," she said.

At the time I spoke to one man from the town who played a video recording over his phone of rapid machine gun fire. He said they were shooting around the corner from his house in the Christian neighbourhood. He said they were Muslim gangs.

"The first weeks of July were awful – men armed with sticks were walking through our neighbourhoods, people were firing machine guns day and night. We couldn't go to the shops to buy food; there were roadblocks on our streets. Our whole neighbourhood was frozen with fear," said the Christian woman. This went on for almost a week before the army entered Qatana on the afternoon of 16 July.

"Thank God the army came back," said the Christian woman when she saw the first soldiers on the streets.

But the relief was short-lived.

Electricity, water and telephone lines were cut as tanks surrounded all entry points to the town during the operation. A curfew was enforced during the hours of darkness. Residents who wanted to leave Qatana could only do so between nine and eleven in the morning, and once they left the town they could not return.

I was prohibited from entering the town at this time. However, I was told by phone that when the army left – five days later – a rally in support of the president took place. A woman told me how music was played in the streets and people threw rice over the soldiers. Unsurprisingly, she was Christian. Other reports, including one by Amnesty International, claimed that hundreds of people were detained in Qatana over those five days. They were those calling for freedom.

The following weekend I stayed overnight in the town to see if people would come out and demonstrate, as they had done before the army entered the town. Aside from a burst of gun fire at about 2am on a Thursday night, no one took to the streets after prayers that Friday. Two tanks backed up by dozens of soldiers manned the main entrance to the town, checking vehicles for arms and passengers for identification. The regime had won this battle in Qatana, but in the following months the protesters would not lie down.

Religion in Syria is an intensely private and sensitive issue. My Sunni Muslim friends say they have gone for years without knowing their friends' religion. However, members of Syrian minorities I know find a person's religion to be one of the first things they need to know about them.

The state has explicitly enforced (as it does in America, Turkey and North Korea) a national spirit, in this case a spirit of resistance against Israel – 'the enemy' – that transcends religious difference. But as it worked so industriously to claim that 'we are all Syrians, regardless of religion', people started to wonder why the state was promoting this very idea, and if there were real differences between those of differing sects.

Ethnic and sectarian fault lines run deep in this highly religiously divided society. Freedom of religious worship is enshrined in the Syrian constitution but the president of the country must be a Muslim. Membership of the Muslim Brotherhood carries a penalty of death. In 2010 the government banned the display of religious messages on vehicles – ironic where the cult of Bashar sees him idolised everywhere you look. A casino that opened only months earlier on the Damascus airport highway and brought significant revenue to government coffers (from Gulf and Iraqi gamblers) was shut down.

Syria's Christians, the majority of whom are from the Eastern Church, find far more in common with their Sunni and Shia countrymen than with the Christians of elsewhere around the world. Unlike many countries with a heterogeneous ethnic population, Syrian identification cards do not state the holder's religious orientation. There is much to tie Syrians together.

It has been the millennia-old constellation of religious and ethnic groups that has made Syria the attractive cultural gem it is today. They bring with them languages, dancing styles, different foods, histories, clothing and experiences that embody humanity itself.

Millions of international Christian and Shia worshippers descend on Syria every year to pray at some of the holiest sites in the world. Yet it may well be these differences that see the country fall into the grip of sectarian and civil war.

As the army began its operation in Qatana, word surfaced of factional fighting that left thirty people dead inside twenty-four hours in the central Syrian city of Homs. The protesters were fighting back. Here you have the army, led by its Alawite officer class, fighting against largely Sunni Muslim protesters.

Yet for Syria's minorities, from the Christians to the Kurds to the Druze, any government in Syria that is not Islamist-oriented will suffice.

The growing violence would see Syria's minorities, twenty-five per cent of the overall population, take the side of the regime. In the first four months of revolt sides had been picked and Syria's minorities, the Christians, Shia, Alawite and Druze, were siding with an increasingly illegitimate Assad regime.

III

LIES, HALF-TRUTHS AND VIDEOS: THE MEDIA AND THE UPRISING

It was from Iran, when protests surrounding the flawed presidential election broke out in June 2009, that the world first saw the grainy phone camera images of pro-democracy activists being gunned down by state forces.

But it was in Syria that mobile phone cameras gave illustration to an entire revolution. Thousands of videos were uploaded to websites throughout the unrest. The initial videos were important in showing both Syrians and the wider world that protests were actually taking place right around the country. The typical etiquette followed by protestors producing videos was to state the date and place of the protest so that the outside world could chart the growth in the number of protests. Corroborating and verifying these hazy videos with my own eyes, or by asking trusted friends, was a personal goal. Attempting to do so, though, was difficult and at times dangerous.

Unsurprisingly, the media played a vital role in determining whether the Syrian uprising would be successful or not. For protestors, activists and eye-witnesses a camera phone and access to websites such as YouTube were vital. For the regime, its use of propaganda and, at times, a well-coordinated campaign reassured many, particularly the country's minorities and those living in Aleppo and Damascus. Its thesis was that Syria (not the regime, mind) was facing an external campaign to destabilise the country. The fact that some elements in the uprising used weapons served the regime with vital ammunition for their claims that they were battling armed gangs.

***

Aspiring foreign journalists who ventured across from Beirut to ply their trade as writers in Syria usually worked for one of *Syria Today, Forward, What's On Syria* or the English publication of *Baladna.*

In *Forward,* where I worked as a freelancer for almost two years, a small team of editors tried hard to present their own view, but with difficulty. Sami Moubayed, the editor-in-chief, said he liked the president very much. Like all Syrians, he thought Syria should get back the illegally occupied Golan Heights. Before the unrest he saw and appreciated the government trying to implement changes. But since then, he and his magazine have been accused of being 'soft' or pro-regime in some quarters. Others, including an official from the Ministry for Foreign Affairs referred to him as "part of the opposition". These contrasting views brought forward an important issue in Syria with regard to all aspects of political debate: you are either with or against – there is no 'maybe', no essential, binding middle ground.

The two main English-language magazines – *Syria Today* and *Forward* – stopped running monthly editions of their respective magazines for a time because revenue from advertising reduced significantly: they had no money to publish. Furthermore, any journalist still left in the country and worth a penny was writing for international outlets instead of the local editions.

Two men in their thirties began their own media campaign to address what was taking place in Syria early on during the unrest. Their campaign to create awareness about 'The Situation' had, by June, been the talk of Damascus.

"We're trying to defuse the anger/fear cycle here; trying to campaign and raise awareness about the middle ground," Ammar Alani, one of the two creators of the campaign that called for citizens to respect the law and to express themselves told

National Public Radio (NPR) in July 2011. The campaign, which saw hundreds of posters calling for calm, could be seen everywhere in Damascus.

But when I met Samir in June, he showed me on his iPhone how his friends on Facebook had jokingly introduced their own versions of the above-mentioned poster campaign created by the two men.

'*Ana ma al-Qanoon*' (I'm with the law) was changed to '*Ana mu Hindi*' (I'm not Indian), Samir showed me with a laugh and a shrug of his shoulders.

Other satirical changes to the official poster campaign included 'I'm with the law, but *where* is it?' and 'Your way is my way, but there's a *tank* in the way', reflecting a widespread public reaction and anger to both the events and to the government's response.

From the outset, *Baladna* and its English-language sister publication of the same title supported the regime. This is hardly surprising when one considers it is owned by United Group, which is in turn owned by Majed Souliman. Majed is the son of Bajhat Souliman, the head of Syria's internal security until 2005.

In September I met the editor-in-chief of *Baladna* English newspaper, Basel Bannoud. On the very same day, the 2011 Syrian uprising was six months old and ten people were killed when security forces stormed a farm near the southern city of Deraa.

United Group's offices in Mezzah are a symbol of modernism and success. The company publishes the popular *Top Gear Syria* magazine as well as a free classified newspaper called *Al Waseeleh*, among others. Walking down the street to their building under the hot sun I passed half a dozen embassies. At the Ukrainian embassy a few young men were holding reams of papers, no doubt keen to get out of the country with job prospects rapidly drying up. When descending the glass stairs into the UG offices underground during my early days as a journalist in 2008, I would be met with the wry stares of half a dozen receptionists busily answering phone calls. The offices were closed that day.

"Before the unrest we had a staff of eight editors and writers, two copy editors and a freelance budget of US$2,000 per month.

Today we have a staff of four, no copy editors and a freelance budget of zero," Basel Bannoud says from *Baladna's* empty offices in a nearby building. His newspaper has been reduced to publishing weekly because there is simply no money available for businesses to advertise any more.

"If you are looking to hear a pro-government opinion," which I was, "you won't hear it from me," he said.

"But you're the editor-in-chief of *Baladna* English; I and everyone else know what line the *Baladna* newspapers have been taking," I responded.

"Yes, but this is not my own personal opinion," he remarked.

"You see all Syrian media is controlled and censored. Every issue of every publication must go to the Ministry for Information; they regularly call me up looking for clarifications if something appears anyway critical of the government," he stated with a sigh.

Basel began by giving me some insight into the extent of government control over the media.

"The way the media and publishing industries work in Syria is like this: when the government announces that it wants a new, independent media, as it did in 2006, it approves licences for those who are linked to the regime. These guys – including the boss of my newspaper – get these contracts. They then staff their newspapers with Christians or Alawites or people from their own families who they know hold a supportive opinion of the regime. And this does not only apply to the media industry – you could say it is the case in any company; anywhere licences are issued. Those who are tied to the regime are simply the ones who are awarded the licences and contracts. It's that simple."

He says that the distribution company is owned and therefore controlled by the regime so that they can decide where the newspaper is sent and when it is stopped, "so sometimes we run a slightly different version," he said. However, customers who subscribe to the newspaper do not get their copies through the distribution company and as a result the content can sometimes be tweaked a little for subscribers, he added.

"Since I've been editor-in-chief the security have come four times to ask about what we have been writing. They don't have people who can read English very well so they mostly ask about the pictures we print. The funniest incident was about a caricature of Dr. Jekyll and Mr. Hyde that we ran around the time the unrest began. Apparently one of the characters was sitting on a throne and resembled in some way the president. I came to my office to find them waiting for me. I told them the caricature was published to highlight domestic violence!"

I asked if the Arabic edition of *Baladna* was staffed by people like him – who do not support the government but stick it out – or if they were genuine supporters.

"When things kicked off we were told by the authorities to highlight corruption, to say that some people were unhappy and that the government had to carry out some reforms – and to mention that it [the government] was in the process of doing this. The editor of the Arabic edition told the authorities that no, he would not do this, that the government was 100 per cent right that the protestors were all stupid. His own personal leanings were so pro-government he didn't want to criticise them even when he was told to do so!"

The editor was fired a few months into the unrest because other employees kept complaining about his personal management style, not because of his stance, said Basel.

"Three times they ran headlines that said 'Syria is fine', I mean what is wrong with them?!"

Basel said the management attempted to kick him out in the early days but because they simply had no one else, they had to leave him in his position.

"Then how can you stay in your job?" I asked. He said many people who were attacked by the security forces or who had information on the regime's malpractices had come to him but he could not publish any of these stories. "Some day I hope to," he said.

When a former colleague of mine, who was Christian, passed through the office I asked her if she had heard anything about the destruction of two churches the previous Friday in Homs. She said she had not. Basel says that if that had actually happened we would know about it by now. "It would be on Dunia television – the whole world would know about it!"

"It's not just the regime that needs changing, it's people's mind-sets," he said. He told me of another fantasy notion being spun by the state's media which some Syrians were taking as fact.

"Just this week I heard four employees talking in the corridor about how in Qatar, Al Jazeera has constructed massive look-a-like models of the cities of Homs and Hama and was broadcasting scenes of soldiers beating and shooting civilians. These employees fully believed that Al Jazeera was doing this in order to make the Syrian government look bad." According to Dunia TV, where the far-fetched lie originated, "Those scenes would be done by directors from the US, France, and Israel."

I asked him who he thought was responsible for influencing the state's media position.

"The gangs – the *shabiha* [ghost], some of them are the guys you would see driving around late at night in Lattakia when you went up there on holidays. They are smugglers and druggies; they are related to the ruling family and for this reason they can do what they want.

"Some of the 'armed gangs' the regime talks about are in fact these guys – their own men; the rest are common criminals who were released following the two amnesties announced last spring [under the cover of releasing political prisoners] – the regime bought their loyalty by releasing them. This worked for a few months but then they asked for money and had to be paid. It is these people, many of them Alawites, who are largely responsible for the killings and beatings; they are the guys who do the torturing. They make up much of the *shabiha*," he posited.

"But finally, it is impossible for people to believe the government's media line. They say there are armed gangs but how come these armed gangs have never appeared before and how have they all appeared at the same time? What's more, when Homs was more or less free for two months and presumably under the control of the armed gangs this summer there was no trouble – there was peace. But when the army came back into the city the day before Ramadan began there was a massive number of deaths and the regime said that was caused by the armed gangs. So when the army came back to Homs so did the armed gangs, and according to the government, it was the armed gangs who did all the killing! How can people believe this?!"

In December 2011, Basil Bannoud published a scathing two-page criticism of the regime in *Baladna's* final edition. "Half the companies I know have closed, workers and employees are being thrown on the streets, unemployment has reached immeasurable levels and we will soon be begging at the mosques' steps and, yet, they have the audacity to say that everything is alright!!"

***

A host of anti-regime media sources sprang up during the first several months of the uprising and the English-language and wider international media lapped up their reports.

One such broadcaster was Barada TV, named after the river that flows through the Syrian capital. Broadcasting from London, this news station was run by a small group of Syrians who opposed the Assad regime. The station's chief editor, Malik al-Abdeh, told an Australian news network that "we've got quite a strong, I would say a very strong following in Syria. For that reason people now trust us." However, the Syrians I spoke to about the broadcaster said that it was "common knowledge" that Barada TV was receiving money from the government of the United States. US embassy cables released by WikiLeaks found that the US State Department funnelled "as much as $6 million to the group since 2006 to operate the satellite channel and finance other activities inside Syria," reported the *Washington Post* in April 2011. As such, Barada TV was tainted by its association with the US government, something that did not sit well with Syrians, especially the 'silent majority'.

The satellite frequency broadcasting Orient TV, a long-standing critic of the regime, was blocked early on, although its owners changed its broadcast frequency on a weekly basis in order to keep its Syrian audience. Internet radio stations were also established to get word out of the unrest.

Other news groups proved far more important and unbiased in the eyes of many Syrians during the uprising. Ugarit News, Sham

Network News and Homs Network News were online video news organs which used YouTube to upload amateur videos on which the world's media broadcasters depended heavily as a source of footage. Major international outlets used stills from these ad hoc YouTube-based news media in their reports.

Created by activists and fuelled by those facing tanks, bullets and attacks on the streets, they were a vital means of conveying information, at first about demonstrations, and later about beatings and killings of protestors, as well as other military activities and operations around the country. Cells of exiled journalists and activists worked from Beirut, acting as connectors between the wider international media and those on the ground in Syria.

As a facilitator, YouTube was probably the single most important tool in providing visual images of what happened when protestors took to the streets. Once the videos, usually never more than a couple of minutes long but regularly graphically violent, reached YouTube, the world could see.

When the Ministry for Communications and Technology reported in February (after the failed 'Day of Rage' but before the first protests took place) that Facebook, YouTube and several other websites were to be made accessible in Syria for the first time since 2008, many saw it as a positive step. For the majority of young Syrians it made little difference to their networking habits as by then they were skilled in using proxies and non-Syrian IP addresses. However, cynics thought the move to openly allow Facebook and YouTube was a ploy by the authorities to monitor people's usage of such social media. Facebook did function as a forum for both pro- and anti-government musings as well as more organised expressions of opinion. It was also monitored by the Syrian authorities who regularly contacted those expressing anger at the regime, asking them into their offices around the country for 'interviews' as a means of intimidation.

Twitter was awash with government snitches and, for me, reporting daily experiences such as seeing the dozen ambulances drive up from the Golan following the 16 May attempt by Palestinians to breach the area was tempered by the fear that those viewing my updates could swiftly get me interned or expelled from the country. On Twitter activists using pseudonyms posted hourly updates of videos and accounts of demonstrations in relative safety.

Significantly, Syria was the first Arab country to have a public 'Internet Army' hosted on its national networks, which openly launched cyber attacks on its enemies. Syrian radio and television stations sought to draw support for the Syrian Electronic Army, a group of internet-literate pro-regime cyber activists that saw it as their mission to defeat outside media organisations portraying false ideas about what was taking place inside the country. For hours each day pro-government radio stations – the vast majority – encouraged people to join the Syrian Electronic Army on Facebook, to attend pro-government rallies and openly espoused vicious attacks on both the international media and foreign governments.

The 'Army' also employed YouTube and Twitter to further its message and succeeded in hacking into the *Los Angeles Times* and *Newsweek* websites in September 2011. By May of the same year it claimed to have attacked fifty websites.

The brother of a famous Syrian actor told me in September how the Electronic Army hacked his brother's Facebook account and posted pro-government statements and photos on his page. The actor, who had met the president several times and supported Assad, took down the photos and comments, but was careful to allow enough time to elapse so as not to set off rumours that he was 'with the opposition' – which he clearly was not.

In August cyber activists supporting the regime stepped up their campaign by creating a website naming 'plot members' on the website 'The Plot Against Syria'. On the website was a list of individuals including leading human rights advocators and journalists. Visitors were encouraged to report plot members or organisations.

The same month dozens of Indian, Russian and Turkish reporters, as well as journalists from several other countries, were invited to Syria to see for themselves what had taken place in Hama. One Russian journalist reported that "Syria has suffered quite a lot of damage, mainly in the area of police stations and government buildings ... Police cars were also destroyed." An Indian journalist reported that "Outside the mayor's office [in Hama], we meet several young Hama residents who freely tell us they hate the Assad regime and want a change. A woman in a burkha tells me security forces target anyone who shouts '*Allah Hu Akbar*'".

When I met a journalist for Brazil's largest newspaper in Damascus in September, he told me how he was met at the airport by the deputy foreign minister, Faisal Meqdad, after being granted a thirty-day journalist visa to enter Syria. He was assigned a minder and said he found it impossible to speak to people. "When I walk up to someone on the street and try to ask their opinion, they see this guy behind me who is clearly from the security and they just wouldn't talk." On 16 September, he went to a protest in Douma, north of the capital, and saw two protestors shot.

The Brazilian journalist also told me the chargé d'affaires from the Syrian embassy in Brazil reads all news about Syria published in Portuguese, indicating the level of surveillance the regime operates overseas. The same official actually flew back to Damascus specifically when the journalist was in town. Two days after visiting Douma he emailed me to say his interview with Syria's foreign minister, Walid al-Mouallim, had been 'cancelled' because of his reporting in Syria, the journalist thought. He would leave a couple of days later.

One Damascus-based diplomat told me how George Baghdadi, a reporter for CBS News, was detained and beaten by security forces. After years as a regular contributor to both news and feature stories from Syria, his by-line swiftly disappeared from the American broadcaster's coverage of the events.

Khalid Oweis, a Jordanian who had worked for Reuters from Syria for five years, was forced to leave the country on 25 March for his "unprofessional and false" news reports on Deraa, as was Suleiman al-Khalidi, also at Reuters. The case of Dorothy Parvaz, who attempted to enter Syria on an expired Iranian passport but was detained and sent to Tehran, raised some eyebrows and fuelled the regime's attacks against Al Jazeera. (No western countries would allow entry to journalists or others with an expired passport, though this lady thought that in Syria she could get away with it.) A swathe of freelancers based in Syria long before the unrest began were denied re-entry to the country or refused renewal of their visas in the early days of the unrest. The Ministry for Information stopped issuing journalist visas as the regime struggled to patch together a narrative.

Established in 1996, Al Jazeera upheld the Palestinian cause, highlighted America's failings in Iraq, laid out Israel's wrongs in the region and Hosni Mubarak's election fraud. From Doha it was beamed into millions of households across the region glad to have an outlet airing their own concerns. Though it remains the voice of the Arab world, its editorial policy when reporting on the Syrian uprising saw its popularity fall among Syrians, especially with the 'silent majority' that was neither with nor against the government.

Usually a disclaimer stating "Al Jazeera is not permitted into Syria" would accompany any news piece the broadcaster carried on the country. Though the images it screened were unverifiable they certainly were emotive. Images of bodies being thrown into rivers or of bloody corpses saw viewers quickly draw their own conclusions.

One Al Jazeera correspondent posted on Twitter in April how he "would have loved to go into the streets of Damascus and speak to people" shortly before leaving the capital.

At the time this was a ridiculous statement. Many foreigners – including foreign journalists like myself – walked the streets of the capital mingling and talking with locals every day. Many foreigners spoke openly with Damascenes about the unrest, in restaurants and cafés around the city.

There were other examples of media discrepancies.

On 14 August, *The New York Times* ran the headline "Syrian Naval ships join attack on coastal city", giving the impression of fact. Two Americans living in Lattakia and with clear views of the sea said though ships were visible, no such gunboat attacks were heard, according to a post on Syriacomment on 25 August.

The New York Times was not alone in this. Dozens of internationally-renowned publications and outlets, including Al Jazeera, did the same.

Other rumours appeared of "armed men spraying bullets" on church walls in the Christian neighbourhoods of Qusoor, Abbasiyeen and Qasaa in Damascus. As I was in close contact with Christians from the area, some told me that shots were fired from a car in Abbasiyeen square days before Easter Sunday and that an anti-regime Christian man attempted to initiate a demonstration at Knesset Solieb (the Church of the Cross) in Qasaa around the same time, but none said any such gun attack on a church took place.

Al Jazeera was culpable of misstating facts when referring to the town of Qatana – which lies a full twenty-eight kilometres from Damascus – as a "suburb of the capital".

A plethora of international outlets mistakenly stated that Al Rai, the television station broadcasting messages by Libya's on-the-run Colonel Gaddafi in the autumn of 2011, was Syrian: the station is based in Syria but owned and operated by Mishan al-Juburi, an Iraqi.

Dozens of Damascenes I spoke to told me they would only watch BBC or Al Jazeera. "This is where we see the truth about our country," one pharmacist, a Sunni, told me in June 2011.

However, many more rural Christians said that they would "never watch those liars again". They showed me video clips of how men would call into Al Jazeera claiming they had either taken part in a demonstration or experienced state brutality only to swear profusely on air at the network for its false reports and coverage of Syria. In August, a Christian friend said of Al Jazeera: "Look, they keep using the same videos; they have been using the same images for the past three days."

Ali, an Alawite acquaintance, told me how he had to reassess his long-held view that Al Jazeera was professional and impartial. "Since we see how they are providing false information about Syria, how do we know what they were reporting about Egypt and Libya was actually true? I know it is important to never believe everything a television channel reports but I thought, because of how they covered the Palestinian-Israeli conflict, that they could be trusted. We can't trust Syrian television or *Tishreen*, so where do we turn to for the right news?"

Al Arabiya, the Dubai-based Saudi news channel, had long been discredited by Syrians for its perceived unbalanced coverage of the region. The majority of Syrians saw it as a tool of the US and Saudi Arabia and little else. But when compared to Al Jazeera's coverage of Syria, many saw it as being more even-handed.

Many English-language media outlets were unashamedly anti-regime, though after ten months of revolt two articles in quick succession condemned this bias. Patrick Cockburn of *The Independent* newspaper wrote on 15 January "suppose that our journalist takes out the word 'rumour' and substitutes 'YouTube' or 'blogger' as the source. Then, going by recent experience, editors will nod it through, possibly commending their man or woman for judicious use of the internet. The BBC and other television stations happily run nightly pictures of mayhem from Syria, grandly disclaiming responsibility for their authenticity. These disclaimers are intoned so often that they now have as much impact on viewers as warnings that a news report may contain flash photography." He continued, "Sadly, al-Jazeera, which has done so much to shatter state control of information in the Middle East since it was set up in 1996, has become the uncritical propaganda arm of the Libyan and Syrian rebels."

Jonathan Steele's article in *The Guardian* on 17 January 2012 was headlined: "Most Syrians back President Assad, but you'd never know from western media." Quoting an, albeit skewed, poll of Syrians conducted by the Doha Debates, Steele noted that 55 per cent of Syrians wanted Assad to stay – largely motivated by fear of civil war. He argued that "The pity is that it was ignored by almost all media outlets in every western country whose government has called for Assad to go" and how "Biased media coverage also continues to distort the Arab League's observer mission in Syria."

***

On 7 September, the day the ambassadors of Italy, Japan and Tunisia returned to their posts in Syria, I met Jihad Yazigi at a downtown café in Damascus. By now, in mid-September, the figures of daily dead across the country had climbed to thirty and forty, though in the capital the rising number and frequency of deaths drew little concern. The initial shock that coloured people's reactions in the spring was long gone.

The air was fresh and damp from the first rains the city had experienced for almost six months. It had given people on the streets a lift, following a difficult Ramadan of fasting through the August heat; the rain – though brief – had also given people something new to talk about. Outside the Four Seasons Boulevard, which houses a chain of café restaurants, hawkers selling sunglasses and chatting with car clampers in the packed car park.

A Syrian, Yazigi was the editor of the Syria Report, an economics and financial data website that charts economic patterns and major business dealings.

Dressed in a suit, he told me he was preparing to travel to the US in a couple of days. For a Christian, he was refreshingly open about what he thought the regime was doing.

"The most important thing about how the Syrian media is presenting the unrest is that you must identify a difference between the state-run publications, for example *Al-Baath*, *Tishreen* and *Thawra*, and the regime publications, such as *Baladna* and especially *Al-Watan*. The first group are very restricted in what they can write – even though they are the state, they feel they have to be careful and cannot or will not take risks. It is not in their nature, it is not in the nature of the Baath party to evolve or to change or to take risks. So everyone who works at these publications just follows the line that has existed for decades. No one wants to speak out, even a little, because they are afraid for their jobs – as workers for the state they have jobs for life and they value this far and away above the morals of journalism." The regime newspapers, including *Al-Watan*, are not restricted by Baath party idealism and are more influenced by the perspectives of those who established them: former security officials or leading regime families.

Yazigi said that he knew several Christian bishops living in towns in central Syria who entirely opposed what the government was doing to protesters but "were afraid to speak out".

"The Christian community is not united in its support of the regime, but many are afraid to speak out – not because they are afraid of being detained by the security services, but because they are afraid of being stigmatised in their communities."

He told me that several Syrians working for international media organisations had come under severe pressure to leave their jobs following threats to their families.

"The most high profile was the case of Samira al-Masalmeh [the editor of *Tishreen* who was fired from her job in April 2011]. She is notorious for changing her opinions for the smallest personal advantage, but she was fired for saying the slightest thing. All she said was that there was a military operation in Deraa, where she is from. This was enough for her to get kicked out of the newspaper."

I asked him why no middle ground media outlet has formed since the beginning of the unrest, something that in avoiding extreme views could appeal to a wider population.

"That's because there is no middle ground – when people are being killed can you put yourself in the middle ground? Of course not!"

***

Well-oiled by decades of anti-Israeli and anti-western propaganda, Syria's state media went into overdrive during the unrest.

SANA, the state-run news agency, published one of many furious articles against Al Jazeera and Al Arabiya, the region's two major Arabic broadcasters, in September 2011, stating:

"The channels also surpassed the stage of receiving calls from 'eyewitnesses' and coercing them to say what they want or outright instructing them on what to say, moving from media instigation against Syria to direct contribution to the acts of the armed criminal groups who commit murder, vandalism, abduction and other crimes against the Syrian people. In their new approach to dealing with Syria, these channels started calling on the international community to intervene in Syria as it did in Libya, demanding that the Security Council impose sanctions." [sic]

The article reported how "Qusai Abdel-Razzaq Shaqfeh, 29, from the central province of Hama, confessed that he had acted as an eyewitness and fabricated false news and videos on events in Syria for the Doha-based al-Jazeera TV channel, and had collaborated with foreign sides to form armed groups to attack the army and security forces and civilians.

"The terrorist also said he had lied about the killing of security members, whose bodies were thrown in the Orontes River when he claimed that those members were killed by other security personnel who put on Hama costumes, in order to accuse Hama inhabitants of the crime. In fact, the gunmen had killed those members and threw their bodies in the river," stated the article.

"Shaqfeh said he received about 2 million Syrian pounds (about US$ 40,000) in instalments from the so-called 'free Hama citizen', whom he later knew to be a relative of Adnan al-Ar' our, a defected Syrian clergyman who used to appear on Arab TV channels to provoke Syrians to demonstrate against the government. He said that the money was used to supply protestors with food and money, and help them to set up the barricades and roadblocks and to buy weapons, including machine guns, for the gunmen [sic]."

State TV offered no evidence or records of such claims. The regime never invited international media outlets to further investigate or to debate these allegations, not even for their own sake.

In September, Hussein al-Harmoush, the army officer who defected after being ordered to tell his soldiers to shoot unarmed civilians, told Syrian state TV in an interview that while he did defect, he was never ordered to shoot civilians. He said he was lured back over the Syrian border by other officers who said they wanted to defect too. He was executed in January 2012 when in the Syrian authorities' custody.

Around the same time Syrian authorities miraculously captured the Israeli spy who was responsible for giving information to Mossad about the Hezbollah military mastermind, Imad Mughniyeh, who was killed when his car exploded in Kafr Souseh, Damascus, three-and-a-half years earlier. What fine timing and intrepid investigation this seemed to be by the authorities – their very existence was being threatened by a growing protest movement and with the army and security services stretched right around the country, they still had the resources to track and find this 'agent'.

Reem Haddad, the director of Syrian state TV for a time during the unrest, tried valiantly and failed totally to articulate the Syrian government's fears and point of view. Her reasoning to the BBC on why there were 5,000 Syrian refugees in tents over the Turkish border in June 2011 would have been comical in other circumstances. They fled, she said, because: "A lot of them [refugees] find it easy to move across because their relatives are there. It's a bit like having a problem in your street, and your mum lives in the next street, so you go and visit your mum for a bit." Her words reflected the simply delusional view held by the regime.

For hours each day the pro-regime Dunia television station broadcast what could only be referred to as fascist propaganda. It displayed images of soldiers and policemen being carried to their graves, others lying in hospitals with nationalist music as a background. It aired emotive videos of people kissing portraits of the president and people cheering the army as it passes through the latest liberated town, now 'free' from the 'armed gangs'. It would then run short news clips showing how the 'Syria is fine' campaign had reached Aleppo and that hundreds of thousands had turned out "in support of President Assad and his reform process".

Dunia campaigned relentlessly against Al Jazeera and Al Arabiya, taking apart their reportage on Syria, dissecting it into possible truths and presenting such 'discoveries' as stone cold fact.

When the state spoke using the word 'Syria' it covertly meant 'the regime'. Following several months of this rhetoric, people grew wise. For the majority it did not mean they would begin supporting the protest movement, but it did lead to a massive wave of discontent growing, especially in Damascus, during August and September. The elevated death count from Ramadan, while not having any immediate effect, served to anger a lot of people, putting them further at odds with the regime.

Blaming 'Islamists' without any element of proof was nothing new to the regime. In April 2004, Islamists were held accountable for an attack in the Mezzah area of the capital. Then, in September 2008, Syrian state television broadcast 'confessions' by a daughter of Shaker al-Absi, the leader of the Islamist group, Fatah al-Islam, who claimed responsibility for an attack on a Palestinian security compound in south east Damascus. It was, said the authorities, an extremist plot working to destabilise the country. And again in 2011 the unrest plaguing the country was the work of Islamist extremists and western governments working hand in hand against Bashar al-Assad – untenable as that might seem.

The nationalistic intensity that saw posters reading 'Get out BBC, Al Jazeera and Al Arabiya!' soon evaporated as summer began. As international outcry grew the posters were replaced, with 'We love the Russian people' or with 'Thank you China' posters appearing around the streets of Damascus.

On consecutive Saturday evenings in March, April and May on my way home I passed by the Al Jazeera Damascus bureau. Each Saturday evening small crowds of young men stood around on the footpath outside the offices chanting their support for the president and ordering the news station out of the country. The groups were being watched and probably organised by three or four policemen who sat on car bonnets, chatting and smoking. One evening in April, the journalist Zeina Khodr reported from the first floor office as young men attempted to break down the main door into the building. A short time later from my vantage point in a microbus I saw a woman on the phone looking out the large glass window at the crowd from the network's first floor bureau. Shortly afterwards the network was shut down and its reporters banned from Syria.

By mid-summer, tension hung heavy in the air. People were being called via SMS messages and email to participate in 'Supporting Syria and President Bashar al-Assad' rallies and concerts. At the same time protests calling for the president's head were multiplying in number and frequency in the provinces.

***

Having worked in the state media, albeit for a period of just eight months, I had gained some insight into how entrenched the government's official viewpoint is and how disinclined it is to change and to move with the times.

My work was censored. Words would be replaced so as to sound less or more critical of the US government, Israel, Iran or certain Lebanese politicians.

At times I would be asked by my editor-in-chief for a synonym for 'infiltrators'. As a good journalist, he did not want to use the same word twice.

"Which is better," he would ask. "'Occupied Palestinian Territories' or 'Illegally Occupied Palestinian Territories'?" or he would say "Jerusalem is not the capital of Israel – it is Tel Aviv! – be careful!"

There was a very structured editorial line that was to be taken. If I overstepped this line I would end up asking day after day for weeks on end when my article would be published. Many of mine never were. The staff at *Syria Times* were polite; perhaps being the only native English speaker at an English publication made me somewhat valuable to them. But, in my role as editor, I clashed with many. "Don't change my articles – it is a matter of style," one opinion writer who regularly submitted the same articles over and over told me. One contributor who wrote a piece about a classical music concert vaulted up the stairs into the room where I worked one day. "Why did you completely change my article?!" he fumed, gripping a copy of the newspaper in his hand. "Because it was not fit for publishing the way it was," I told him. "I lived in Scotland for thirteen years and worked as a doctor – I know English!" he said. With that, he was off.

Some of *Syria Times'* editorial positions were, I felt, fair: charting the awful consequences of the American invasion in Iraq, Israel's disingenuous efforts at peace talks with Palestinians and international tinkering in Lebanon were all important issues on which western governments were criticised.

But the basic thesis of the newspaper was such that no one in their right mind – not Syrians nor foreigners – would pick up the newspaper to read it, except, perhaps, for the full English translation of the speech by Bashar al-Assad following his 're-election' in 2007 or to get the results of the Syrian football league (at the time the Homsi team, Karama, were doing well in the Asian Champions League).

Headlines would read: "President Bashar al-Assad meets team of Malaysian businessmen, focuses on brotherly relations" or "Iranian deputy minister for local housing thanks President Assad for telephone call" or even "World leaders send telegrams to President Assad congratulating him on his re-election".

Jihad Yazigi argued that the state-owned and run publications, *Baath*, *Tishreen* and *Thawra*, were far more restricted in what they could publish because every time an idea was discussed, the first question to be addressed was "How will it reflect the position of the party?" Yazigi was right about this, but at *Syria Times* it was the atmosphere as much as the people who filled the offices that conspired to drain any inclination towards creativity: this was first and foremost a job for life for those who worked there, a distant second was that it was a newspaper and that journalistic integrity was required.

So for this reason the English and Arabic language state newspapers continued to run the same drivel for years on end, with a negligible readership, in spite of them costing just five Syrian pounds (10 US cents).

***

Basel Bannoud of *Baladna* English had told me that if I wanted to hear the regime's side of the story I should speak to a colleague of his. On 19 September, I did so. Sari Akminas, a senior editor at the newspaper, met me outside a cigarette shop in the Souk Sarouja neighbourhood in central Damascus around 7pm. The sun had just dropped beyond the horizon but the summer's warmth remained in the air. Before 2009, Souk Sarouja was a grimy, enclosed part of the city where foreign backpackers would stay at one of two Lonely Planet-endorsed hostels before taking the short walk to the Old City out past hawkers selling posters of Cristiano Ronaldo and pirated DVDs, amid loud *dabke* music. Since then, however, lower-middle class Damascenes have returned to the area in droves.

On this Monday night the quarter was alive with revellers. Crowds in the hundreds sat outside in the narrow alleyways smoking *argeleh* water pipes and chatting. Waiters brought tea and side dishes of hummous and *fool* (fava) beans to hungry young Damascenes. Souk Sarouja is not a place to find the city's wealthy; they are at the cafés next to the Four Seasons hotel and in the upscale neighbourhoods of Malki and Abu Roumanieh. Sarouja now carries with it a reputation as a home for the city's young, hip, alternative crowd.

A twenty-five-year-old Circassian who lived in Rukn Eldeen in northern Damascus, Sari began to tell me about what had happened in Barzeh, an area in north east Damascus, that saw violent clashes between security forces and demonstrators in the spring and early summer of 2011.

"Barzeh is half poor and half middle class," said Sari. "The second Friday [of protests] there was a confrontation between the security and protestors at a major square in the neighbourhood. I looked down and saw gun shots and then the security men running away in all directions. This means they must have been shot at; it was their natural response.

"For the next few Fridays no one could go out; you couldn't even open your windows. There were shootings every evening until about 8pm and at exactly midnight people would start the *takbir* (calling 'Allah u Akbar') right across the neighbourhood."

The alleyways were even more packed by now with people streaming up and down, akin to the narrow side streets of Istanbul.

"Sometimes Syrian TV broadcasts interviews of guys with their shirts buttoned up to their necks, so we know these guys are probably black and blue under their shirts. This is happening. But everyone knows the media in Syria is a lot freer than it was in the past. For example *Al-Watan*, though it is owned by Rami Makhlouf, has published things people never thought they would see in print in Syria. It was revolutionary when it came out first [in 2006]," he said.

"The president said himself that the security forces don't know what to do when they see people shouting 'freedom, freedom', they only know one way to react and that is to attack them."

"But if he is the president, the boss, why can't he simply call the security in?" I asked.

Sari shrugged his shoulders, lighting another cigarette.

I asked Sari what percentage of the protestors was armed gangs; he said he thought about 90 per cent.

"I think there is no place for being in a grey area with regard to the media or the situation. You have to be a man and come down on one side or another."

I asked him about the Circassian or Adyghe community in Syria, who, as Muslims, fled the Russian Caucasus in the 1860s after the defeat of a long uprising.

He said the Circassian community, which numbered about 250,000 in Syria, were supportive of the regime; I took this to be because of their minority status. "When people come out of the mosques on Fridays they have been listening to the sheikh and after his sermon they are filled with the ideas he talks about. So if he says the government is bad then they will go outside and protest against the regime."

Was Sari pro-regime because of his background? Most likely.

The same day I met a group of Syrian friends; all men and in their mid/late-twenties. I wanted to know what they thought of the media's portrayal of the unrest. They were more interested in talking about East-West values, the meaning of life, and philosophy than the media. One of the group, Khaled, said his father was at the powerful Rifae mosque in Kafr Souseh, the day its sheikh, Osama Rifae, was beaten by the security on 27 August.

"My father said there were lots of security men outside around the mosque. When people came out some started shouting '*Allah u Akbar*' and some started throwing empty glass bottles at the security. Then the security forces attacked the people and the sheikh, who was outside, was beaten. My father said the sheikh wasn't targeted, but was among the protestors."

Fascinating as this was, I wanted to hear what they thought of the media. "Al Jazeera is lying, Syrian television is not showing the truth either," said Aboud, a dentist, who watched Al Jazeera, Dunia, the BBC and Syrian state television for news.

My friend, Samir, said that "people really hate Al Jazeera. All they show is news about how many people have been killed each day; all they do is focus on the numbers and take phone calls from people demonstrating. At least BBC and Al Arabiya are giving voices from both sides a chance to talk but Al Jazeera doesn't do this. It doesn't broadcast any news about things the government is trying to do – the attempts to change the parties and media laws, or about the new election law that the government announced".

Samir said he was totally against the government's actions and was disgusted by the fact that there were Syrian refugees "sleeping under Turkish stars" but added that "the job of the media is to show both sides but Al Jazeera talks about one side and that that's it".

Aboud called me aside and said he had something to tell me. "I know what is going to happen. In about four months the leading opposition members will come to Damascus and hold a meeting with the prime minister and they will discuss the political parties issue. We will then have parliamentary elections early next year [2012]. I heard this from the son of the country's top intelligence man – from his own lips."

Their interest quickly waned. It was, for them, a subject they had long since tired of.

IV

THE GAP BETWEEN STATE AND SOCIETY

It was mid-September 2011 when I invited some Christian friends for dinner at a friend's farm outside the restive town of Qatana. It was a beautiful late summer's evening. Daytime temperatures had subsided and in the now quiet Christian neighbourhoods families and elderly residents sat out on the streets smoking, drinking tea and chatting. On the way to the farm, located in an informal settlement area populated mostly by Alawite families, we were stopped at two checkpoints each backed up by four tanks camouflaged with tree branches and military ponchos, and decorated with images of the president. A young soldier looked at our driver's ID card and waved us on. Several tanks had their guns pointed at residential houses, Christian houses. One man present at the farm, a government official at the time, had helped me re-enter the country two weeks earlier. Some of those present were from Homs. All spoke of the awful things 'extremist Muslims' were doing both in Homs and right there in the town of Qatana. Another from Qatana said a bullet had become lodged in his front door several weeks earlier. One of the two from Homs retold how the demonstrators had blocked off streets in four parts of the city and people were afraid to go out after dark.

The protest movement in Qatana reached its zenith in July with the announcement of a new emir and the establishment of an Islamic emirate. The army then moved in and arrested dozens of people. Hundreds more – Christian, Sunni and Druze – fled the town. One of the dinner guests said that when this happened he took his family out of the town and returned himself to keep watch over his elderly parents and the family home. On his drive back into the town he was stopped by a man with a gun and a scarf over his face who ushered him up a side street. The edgy gunman said that my dinner guest had to drive very slowly, otherwise the car would be shot at by snipers on the roofs of surrounding houses. The Christian man was convinced these people were Islamic terrorists though, in reality, they could have been regime enforcers.

The government official, whom I cannot name and who was also Christian, said: "The army didn't move in until things got very bad." Though the situation deteriorated for a time following the troop deployment, this point was true: I was in the town only days before the army moved on Qatana in July 2011. There were violent street clashes and shootings between Alawites and Sunnis.

"There are three kinds of demonstrators," said the official. "One group have legitimate problems and concerns and they have every right to protest in the streets – they are protesting because they do not have enough food, money or jobs. The second group are those who are throwing stones at police and are calling for the end of the regime. The third group are those who are funding the protests, by giving money to people to cause mayhem," he said.

He went on, "For example in Douma, a local businessman paid another man 200,000 Syrian pounds [slightly over US$4,000] to shoot at protestors. The man said that as he was poor he would do it. So one Friday after noon prayers the man went to the top of one building where a gun was waiting for him and he shot the leading demonstrator in the crowd below. He missed but fired at a second person who fell to the ground."

He told me to go to his office the following day to give collect some DVDs of "what the gangs are doing".

I suggested that one good thing to have emerged out of the unrest was that people were now talking more freely and expressing their opinions. He agreed, though he added that there were many problems facing Syrians. "What makes people angry is that while they sit in traffic the government or army cars drive straight through the red light," I said. He nodded his head.

I asked him about Iran: "The relationship between Syria and Iran doesn't make sense. Iran is an Islamic, Shia country. And it is Persian – it's not even Arab – so why is Syria friends with Iran? It doesn't make sense."

He agreed, before continuing, "Listen, I'll tell you something sort of secret. When I was working in D.C. during the last decade we were told to reach out to the Americans and to grow ties. The Americans said they were interested in security issues, namely, securing our border with Iraq – which we largely did as they had asked. We said we want to focus on other issues, on trade, on education, on diplomacy but they never took us up on anything except the security issue. The Israel lobby was too strong. So when someone comes to us – Iran – offering trade deals and warmer ties, it suits the Syrian Arab Republic to work with them. What else could we do when the Americans had no interest in helping us develop? The [Syrian] president is a big fan of the American president and he realises how American businesses could help educate our country, but they just wanted things their own way."

I met the official at his office in Kafr Souseh in Damascus the next day, as we'd discussed. Outside, people scrambled to and from offices looking for government stamps. Some wanted to travel; others were seeking permission to marry. I was reminded that though this Ministry's offices were impressively large and modern, the system within appeared antiquated.

The official was due to travel to the embassy in Washington in two days. Through his government position he spent a lot of time with cabinet ministers with important portfolios, he said.

"There are lots of people with problems in Syria; we know this. But change takes time," he said, reaching for the DVDs.

"We need democracy but not from outside [overseas]. We have extremists and radicals in our country – we cannot base a Syrian model of democracy on examples from other countries."

"When the situation in Deraa began back in March I spoke to a well-known sheikh from the town and told him to bring a dozen other respected people to the Ministry to talk about the situation. I also asked him to bring a group of young people. When they came I asked one man, he was twenty years old, what he wanted. He said he wanted freedom. I asked him to explain what he meant exactly. He said he wanted to be able to smoke in front of his father without being punished; he said he wanted the freedom not to go to school or to listen to his headmaster. He said he didn't want to have to do military service."

"Is this what you call freedom?" the official asked me. "They don't know what freedom is!"

"And how many soldiers and security men have been killed trying to protect people and trying to maintain order in the country?" he added. I didn't disagree.

"What we are concerned about now is how the regional countries will react," he went on. "The reforms need time. We will have parliamentary elections in February [2012] and people will be able to choose themselves."

I tentatively raised the subject of presidential elections – from my face I guess he knew that would be my next question. "The president's term is up in 2014 and though we are unsure now, we expect there to be presidential elections then, when his term is up. Why not? This [i.e. the regime's arbitrary practices] is what we are trying to change."

He handed me the DVD copies and left me with a warning.

"The Syrian army is very strong – we have used 10 per cent of our resources to keep control over the gangs and criminals but the army has a lot in reserve."

State and society have always been divided in Baathist Syria, most simply and effectively because of the former's desire to control all spheres of life. This is perhaps best represented by Article 8 of the 1973 Syrian constitution which declares that the Baath party is the "sole leader of state and society in Syria". This condition made it illegal for organic political movements and parties to grow, develop and contribute to Syrian social and economic life over the decades. When Bashar al-Assad was sworn in in 2000 some attempts were made to wean the country off the state's support structure, but shaking off decades of control proved extremely difficult and, by 2011, it was the state that needed the people.

Employees who worked in the Central Bank of Syria governor's office told me in June 2011 how a campaign was underway to ask employees to contribute 500 Syrian pounds (US$12) of their monthly salary to support the government during the uprising. I doubt many did. The same employees told me how the governor, Adib Mayaleh, would draw rings, question marks and lines through reports submitted to him by employees. He was, apparently, a workaholic and a perfectionist, but he was clearly frustrated by the quality of work he was receiving.

And why wouldn't he be?

Apathy among the state employees I knew grew to become a dark cloud in their consciousness. They earned, on average, about US$270 per month. Few of the rank and file could afford cars, but the state, to its mind, took care of this by using the hulking, uncomfortable 1960s buses to take employees to and from work. The buses had no air conditioning for the summer months and their windows were broken and unable to keep out the cold wind and dirtied rainwater in winter. Central Bank of Syria employees were perhaps the most frustrated group of Syrians I had met during the four years I had been there. On their salaries they could never eat out in restaurants, they could certainly not visit Lebanon or Turkey for holidays. In fact, few took holidays at all as they could receive several hundred Syrian pounds for 'cashing in' these days off. Their workloads, they said, were enormous and many worked seven-day weeks for months on end.

They were simply stuck. There was no progression to look forward to; the past must be swiftly forgotten.

Meanwhile, senior employees such as directors, who arrived to such posts by virtue of being employees of the state for decades – their first and only jobs – were given locally produced Sham cars to drive with fuel paid for by the state.

Working at *Syria Times* when I first came to Damascus first was, and remains, my most startling experience of life in the public sector. We shared an entire floor with the state-run Arabic newspaper, *Tishreen*, and interaction between the staff of both was regular. I would arrive at around 4.30 in the afternoon and sit in a large room consisting of four aged desks and a pile of sun-damaged newspapers in one corner. Mohammad Darwish, an ageing Palestinian man and my sports editor colleague, smoked the foul-smelling Syrian-made *Hamra* cigarettes. Within a few minutes of my arrival he would call for tea or coffee to be delivered to us by one of the three tea boys employed. The tea boys had a boss, the man who ran the tiny 'canteen'. He had no real work to speak of. So four people were employed in this little venture. There were also two day and two night door men. A car or bus transported employees to and from home. This employed two more men who would drive only in the morning and evening but would remain smoking and chatting all day.

Many of the managers (they could not be referred to as editors) for both *Syria Times* and *Tishreen* did little more than watch television. They were polite and asked me in to watch football and drink tea with them occasionally. There was a significant number of female staff at both newspapers. At *Syria Times* – an English-language newspaper – only two people could speak English to any comprehensible extent.

In another room sat a team of translators. Some were long-time employees, others were young, recently graduated English literature students from Damascus University – versed in Shakespeare but inept when it came to news writing. Almost every day they would roughly and carelessly translate one hundred-word notes about how Israel had violated Lebanese airspace or how Gaza was under siege or how the Americans were stealing oil from Iraq. They were more concerned with gossip and office politics. Some mocked the regime using furtive innuendo. Only Mohammad spoke English to me. He would incessantly ask for synonyms for a variety of sports-related words. Football English was lost on him. There was time to pass on to him the phrases 'backs to the wall', 'eating up time' and 'flapped at Messi's incisive pass', but never enough time to explain them.

Almost all the workers at the newspapers were there because of *wasta* (contacts). Most were Alawite and had zero experience of journalism, even less of the English language.

The memory that stays clearest in my mind is the smell of the offices. The bathroom had holes in the roof and floor. All the windows were broken. There was no running water and, needless to say, no soap or paper towels. Because it was the state's responsibility it was allowed to pass into wretchedness.

The working environment was not fit for livestock, never mind journalists. But, as employees of the state – some for decades, guarding the financial security it brought – people accepted it.

The number of properties owned by the state around the country was staggering. In rural areas the government owned huge areas of land occupied by the army. In the cities its portfolio included dozens of buildings left behind by the French that today serve as police offices, warehouses and centres for the security services.

I often reflected to myself that if the government sold only a small percentage of the property it owned, much of which consisted of derelict warehouses or open spaces, it would make a considerable profit given the high cost of property in the capital. Instead buildings and properties were left to fall derelict over the decades. The state's equipment was also clearly decades old. Nor was there investment in the police housing complexes and soldiers' barracks. Unfortunate families lived there in ugly, paint-stripped and underserviced constructions that baked in the summer sun and dripped with damp after the winter and spring rains. Traffic police officers would earn little more than US$200 per month but, I was told, would secure 'services' from shops in the area they worked. They would get free cigarettes, biscuits, water and tea from the nearby supermarket, and the bribes they were offered by vehicle drivers, and took, also helped them and their families get by.

The Central Bank of Syria at Sabah Bahraat appears impressive from the outside but its interior has not been renovated since the 1970s. Similarly, the Ministry for Information in Mezzah, which also hosts the *al-Baath* newspaper and which I regularly visited for journalist visa work, is a pungent, stale edifice.

When I visited the Ministry in early 2011 to renew my visa, I spotted a cockroach climbing over notebooks next to the hands of the receptionist. The man, smoking the mandatory Syrian cigarette while chatting, was entirely unaware.

Before new elevators were installed in late 2011 one had to wait for up to a half an hour to go up or down the floors of the building. As my friend, Samir, who once accompanied me to the Ministry, said: "The minister never sees the problems here. When he arrives his private elevator is waiting for him and the route to his office on the tenth floor is modern and clean."

Consequently, from an aesthetic perspective, the state represented the old, the decayed elements of life, as computer shops displaying sleek Sony laptops and western restaurants and cafés sprang up around them.

The government would typically hand out salary increases to state employees at the end of Ramadan when Muslims buy gifts for the Eid holiday or when fuel increases were introduced, in order to appease the masses. State-run newspapers and other media would then incessantly praise the president for his generosity.

Syria is replete with examples of the state's unconstructive impact on society.

When I interviewed the Syrian actor Duraid Laham, one of the best-known actors in the Arab world in 2010, for a magazine feature, he lamented how when the state got its hands on the cinema industry in the 1960s and 1970s, it fell apart. "They [the government] would buy up rights to the cheapest films available", which they would show in Damascus' shady and shoddy cinema theatres. "No one would want to go see these films. The state took control of the industry and because of the quality screened, no one visited and as a result it had no money to invest properly in film."

During the early stages of the unrest in the spring of 2011, Laham's image could be seen on billboards and posters around Damascus calling for "calm and respect for the law".

Laith Hajo, who has produced political satire series such as *Buqat al-Dow* ('Spotlight') and *Diaa Dia'a* ('The Lost Village'), is one of Syria's most popular directors. A softly-spoken and professional man whom I've had the opportunity to observe working more than once, Hajo's brother was beaten during an "artists' protest" in July 2011. In the past Laith would tell me how when he needed to discuss the script for *Diaa Dia'a* – a slap-stick comedy that touches upon the police state and is based on the lives of a coastal village in northern Syria – with its writer, he had to travel to Belarus to meet with him. Hajo reportedly told a Lebanese news agency that he would cover the unrest in Syria in some of his future work.

The thousands of people who came to Damascus' Umayyeen square on 17 July to celebrate the eleventh anniversary of the swearing in of President Bashar al-Assad were drawn there because the popular singers George Wassouf, Ayman Zbib and Wafik Habib were performing for the crowd. Wassouf, a Syrian Christian from a village not far from Homs in central Syria, regularly charged upwards of US$200 a ticket for his concerts. Amazingly, Zbib is not even Syrian. The Lebanese singer performed at numerous 'people's parties in support of President Bashar al-Assad' around the country and in Damascus during the summer of 2011. A well-known Arabic pop singer, his presence ensured decent turnouts – enough for the SANA and state television cameras to give the impression of broad popular support for the regime.

Hasan, a friend who attended the Umayyeen party, said shortly after that "all the guys went to see the girls and all the girls went to see George Wassouf. No one went for the president. People started using the president as an excuse [to get things], for example, people would say 'If you love the president give me this or that.'" He said he saw many women being groped by men. "Here is not like Europe, when guys get a chance to be close to a woman, they take it!" Assad was not present.

The Syrian composer and pianist Malek Jandali told me how his parents' house in Homs was broken into and how they were tied up, supposedly by government security forces, in July 2011. He believed the state's influence and control of the music and arts scene damaged the normal growth of natural musical talent in Syria. "Because most of the funding for Syrian art, TV and drama comes from the government, there will undoubtedly be limitations on how artists can express themselves. This is counter to the true nature of art, where artists should be free to express themselves as they see fit and make art/music that truly reflects and inspires their communities and societies," he said.

Jandali refused to back the regime and when his family in Homs was attacked, he became a foremost opponent to the regime overnight. "For me, the issue was not political, but humanitarian. I could not stand by and be silent while innocent civilians, even children, were being tortured and killed," he said via email. "A government killing its own people is unconscionable, regardless of one's politics, religion or beliefs. Therefore, in good conscience, I cannot support any government that justifies the killing of its own people, especially innocent children. This is a crime against humanity and it is unacceptable any time anywhere."

When I met Syria's culture minister, Riad Ismat, in June 2011 for an interview with *Forward* magazine, he was at pains to stress that chaos would lead nowhere and that, as President Assad had said in an earlier speech, the government had to respond to the will of the people.

One of the issues I raised with him – in light of this statement – was that many young Syrians love rap and graffiti. "Are there any plans to address what may be viewed by young people as a gap between what young people want and what the state is providing in terms of cultural activities?" I asked.

His longwinded answer, in part below, offers an insight into the gap between state and society in Syria:

> I think there is a major misunderstanding regarding this issue. When the Royal Shakespeare Company (RSC) or Britain's Royal National Theatre (RNT) produce Shakespeare, for instance, they do not produce his works as school assignments, but in a very innovative way and with fresh interpretations that reflect our current times and that address the new generation. In Syria, we try to produce all different kinds of culture, each targeting a different age and standard of education, whether children or pensioners, whether elite or regular people. On the other hand, needs – rather than demands – of the younger generation should be taken into serious consideration, because they are the majority of our audiences. Recently, I requested a repeat of the Ballet School show in the Opera House, which was supposed to be annual, but stopped

since I left my post as Rector of the Academy of Dramatic Arts in 2002, eight years back; I managed to revive this tradition again when I became minister in 2010. Also, I requested a repeat of the Jazz chorus show, which I attended personally in Dummar's Cultural Centre; I asked the Russian instructor Victor Babenko to include more songs in Arabic beside his English repertoire, which he and the ensemble promised to do gladly. Maria Arnaout, the talented violinist and DG of the Opera House, played Dalida's Helwa 'Ya Baladi', with Mayas Yamani and their 'Maqam Troupe' to bring tears to the eyes of the Syrian audience, who gave their performance a standing ovation. That was only one activity of dozens in Hannibal Saad's 'Cultural Landscapes' in Al-Assad Complex for Culture & Arts. The Academy of Dramatic Arts produced two superb productions of modern dance this year, choreographed by Mutaz Malatiali. Very soon, we are scheduling a Syrian Jazz/Rap concert in Arabic by Rasha Rezq and her company, by Lena Chamamyan and her ensemble and by another popular hard rock group. On the other hand, I requested Juan Karajoli to re-establish the Arabic music ensemble and perform our heritage for young audiences. The Experimental Theatre is back, beside the Damascus National Theatre, after decades of silence and negligence; it operated by producing two productions as parallel fringe stream side-by-side with the main stream. Our plan is to strike a balance between what the young people request and what we need to let them acquaint with in order to cultivate a refined taste. Culture should be able to draw wider audiences to its standard, instead of giving compromises to the common taste.

A great deal about Shakespeare, then, and about "our heritage", but not much about rap. No mention of graffiti. Even more instructive is the almost total control the state holds in a sector of social activity – the arts – deemed to be far down the list of government priorities, certainly for a government fighting an uprising.

***

But how much has this growing gap between the Syrian state and its society contributed to the uprising?

The spate of concessions following the mass public demonstrations offered by the government appeared, at first, to be extraordinary moves by the authorities.

It offered 300,000 Kurds citizenship, meaning passports and a consequent ability to travel, it allowed opposition elements to meet, it declared an end to emergency laws, fuel prices were reduced and Syrian television admitted anti-government protests were taking place around the country (though these were swiftly portrayed as being attended by rioters and bandits). Compulsory military service was reduced from twenty-one to eighteen months. Two separate amnesties were issued for political prisoners.

"Syria is a country still technically in a state of war with a neighbour that stole and occupied part of its territory – of course the country needs emergency laws. We are at war, don't forget," a friend once said.

On 25 July, Syrian state media reported that the government approved a new political party law – the first since 1963.

The bill stipulated "the essential objectives and principles governing the activities of parties, conditions for their establishment ... and rules relating to their financing, their rights and their obligations. It prohibits parties founded on the basis of religion, tribal affiliation, regions and professional organisations as well as those which discriminate on the basis of race, sex or colour," according to SANA, the state-run news agency.

Parliamentary elections were to take place by the end of the year, the deputy foreign minister said during a visit to South Africa in August. It never happened.

The closing statement of the government-sponsored Consultative Meeting for National Dialogue in Damascus, which took place between 10 and 12 July and saw 152 individuals from all sides of the political and social spectrum, called for: "A recommendation to set free all of the detainees, who weren't proved to be guilty by judicial authorities during recent events ... recommending the establishment of a higher council for human rights in Syria ... speeding up [the creation of a] corruption fighting mechanism ... The liberation of the Golan is considered among the fundamental causes and national objectives which represents a national consciousness." [sic]

There were other points to the statement, but those above give us a clear sense of the perspective of those who took part in the meeting.

One person present, a friend, laid out his thoughts to me about what took place over the three days:

> The National Dialogue Consultative Meeting was a turning point in the crisis, no doubt, and a milestone that could have been used brilliantly by the opposition. They failed to do so, and the radicals within the Baath insisted on drowning what was said in it, making the conference effectively no longer important. They [the opposition] boycotted it, however, arguing that no dialogue can take place unless the violence ends. I think they missed a golden opportunity, and platform to speak their mind and appeal to the widest possible audience that was watching the meeting live on Syrian TV. That was one of its shortcomings, and so was the attitude of the hard line Baathists, who refused to even accept the fact that Article 8 of the Constitution was a major issue that needed to be cancelled. Their attitude was clear by the barrage of criticism that they levied against us, the independents [those not associated with the government nor out and out activists], through unions, syndicates, press and so forth, in the days after the meeting. What is important about the conference is that it paved the way for a new generation of independent young men and women – fresh, brave, open-minded and reform-oriented. Many of them premiered at the event, spoke their views with no restraints, and managed to change the course of sessions on the second day of the conference, and actually drowned the final communiqué that was due to be issued, which was colourless, tasteless, and poor – to say the least. Instead they lobbied with the rest in the room, petitioning Vice-President Shara, and said that only a new resolution would be accepted by them, one that acknowledged the internal opposition as 'part of the social fabric,', they called for an end to the violence, demanded a new constitution. Had the opposition been around, there is not a thing they would have said that differs from what the independents already did at the conference.

The three-day meeting was broadcast on Syrian state television and heard opinions very rarely expressed through a state-owned media outlet. Many people I spoke to were shocked to hear such criticism of the government articulated. It could have been a watershed moment for the regime – a moment by which they could have genuinely begun to convince the Syrian population that they were serious about the reform process. Broadcasting the conference, with the opinions heard there followed by further gestures of change and accountability, would have helped bring millions of Syrians – many among the 'silent majority' firmly to the side of the government.

But within hours Syrian television had returned to the infiltrators, foreign elements, armed gangs rhetoric. The insecurity, fear and narrow-mindedness of the regime overpowered any sentiment for grabbing the opportunity to maintain their hold on power.

***

Noor called me up on a warm July evening. "I need to see you. Can we meet in an hour?" she asked. I was out of town at the time, so we arranged to meet the next day at 5pm. The following day I took a taxi to Sham City Centre, a large mall in the wealthy Kafr Souseh area of the capital. When I arrived she was waiting in a Daihatsu 4x4 with her sister. Noor told me we were going to see a friend of hers, whose husband had been caught and detained by the security forces the evening before.

We drove across town to the northern neighbourhood of Rukn Eldeen. Noor chatted about university – she still had one exam to sit a month later, English narrative. She complained about the speed of the internet connection in Damascus: "The only thing I can access is Skype." The government had intentionally slowed internet connections across the country so as to inhibit people from uploading videos of regime brutality and anti-government protests, she claimed.

We made our way through heavy afternoon traffic past sweet shops, *shawarma* stands and brittle Saba taxis, and across the President's Bridge from where you can see Damascus sweep up the southern side of Qasiun Mountain. Men sitting on the sides of streets attempted to sell illegally imported cigarettes, their gazes set on the faces of female drivers in passing BMWs. Children flitted between car windows seeking spare change. University students, arm-in-arm, gaggled and laughed. A chorus of beeping ascended from the street whenever the traffic lights turned green. Pulling into a side street on the foothill of Qasiun

I began to wonder if what I was doing was such a bright idea. I asked if the house was safe. Both Noor and her sister said yes simultaneously. By this stage I had turned off my mobile phone and I had previously stashed my USB memory stick at a friend's house. If I was going to be caught, the authorities would not find the USB – all my writings for *The Times* and *Sunday Times*, *FT*, the *Washington Post* and the chapters of this book were saved on it.

We got out of the car and went into an apartment block. The sign outside the sixth floor flat read: 'Eiad Shurbaji – Journalist'.

The apartment, full with children's toys, a small swimming pool and a half-full fish tank, had a view spanning almost the whole of Damascus.

Inside were Ola and Riham. Ola's husband, Eiad, had attended the artists' demonstration in Midan the evening before. Now he was gone. "They went with pens, but thirty-five of them didn't come back."

Riham, a director and aspiring film-maker, said she took a camera to the demonstration but the police acted so quickly she didn't have an opportunity to film anything. Ola said that many were beaten by the plain-clothes security forces.

Ola broke off to take a phonecall. I asked Riham if she thought there would be major problems if the regime were to fall; whether Syria's different religions might go to war. She said yes, there probably would be problems, and by saying so she was the first activist I had met to concede this. She refused to go into any further detail about how or why this might happen.

I looked around for signs of overt religiosity. Voices from my Christian friends, who constantly harped on the threat of the Muslim Brotherhood, were bearing heavily on my mind. Here all but one, Noor, were wearing the hijab, the Islamic headscarf.

However, on the walls were several period paintings of medieval European scenes. Ola tells me how she and Eiad had given her daughter a French name.

"We have no problems with the other religions in Syria. Our problem is with Bashar and the groups around him. Alawites are good people – and Bashar is not the entire Alawite community, he shames them," said Ola.

They talked with much love about Ahmad and Mohammad Malas, twenty-eight-year-old twins and well-known theatre actors.

Ola told me that the new media law proposed as part of the government's reform package was farcical. "They drafted a new law but they didn't ask for input from a single independent journalist."

Eiad founded and edited a popular newspaper called *Shabablek*, which, Ola said, had been critical but fair in its commentary on the regime in the past.

As she sat on the arm of the sofa next to me she continued to update a Facebook page calling for a protest outside the Ministry of the Interior later that same evening.

She said it was impossible to know how many people were at the demonstration as the security forces were present and broke it up before people could gather. Three big buses and two thirty-two-seaters filled with pro-government supporters had swarmed the area.

According to Syrian media, the film director Nabil Maleh and the writer Rima Fleihan were also detained during the protest, which was held opposite Midan's al-Hassan Mosque on 13 July. Others detained during the artists' protest included May Skaf, a prominent actress who had appeared in numerous Syrian series and had been known as a government critic.

What was instructive was the fact that, when asked, Ola knew almost none of the country's so-called leading pro-freedom figures personally, highlighting the spontaneity and genuinely organic nature of the protest movement.

These were normal Syrians who, because of the regime's brutality on peaceful protesters, had turned against the state.

A sit-in had now been arranged by friends and family of those detained. Louma Skaf, sister of May, said its purpose was to "show the authorities that they cannot continue crushing peaceful demonstrations while talking about reform and national dialogue"

The sit-in in front of the Ministry for the Interior would have ushered in the fifth month of the uprising.

A few minutes later Ola received a call from a friend who owned a shop in Merjah square in downtown Damascus close to the Ministry for the Interior. "There are two government buses there already, they know what is being planned," said Ola, her bright blue eyes burning, her plans quickly going up in smoke. As well as the buses, police with batons were reported, and she decided, after several phonecalls and Facebook posts, to call off the protest.

"What was the regime thinking? That it could arrest every single person who takes to the streets?" one of the women said.

I reminded them that if the regime were to go, then civil war was very possible in Syria, that everyone would fight against each other out of sectarian fear.

"Listen, you should know something. Sunni, Shia, Christians, Alawites, Druze and so on lived in peace and without problems long before the Assads came to power. The Assads are not Syria – they are not the country. Syria has an immense history and these gangsters are only a speck on this," she retorted. "This is an idea the Syrian people need to take back."

I walked through the streets after leaving the house of women. Down through Jisr al-Abiad, dozens of street stalls had been illegally set up since the unrest began and many Chinese men and women were now plying their trade selling trinkets, scarves and jewellery. I thought about the women and Ola's eighteen-month-old daughter, Julia, and reflected that the same scene must have been taking place in dozens or hundreds of homes right around the country. But where were the men in that house? Perhaps in hiding or already detained by the authorities.

At that point I was never more convinced that the regime would fall.

Noor called me again, five days after our visit to Eiad Shurbaji's home, to say "my friends have come back from their trip". She meant that the actors and writers who protested and were detained the previous Wednesday had been released; Eiad, along with twins Mohammad and Ahmad Malas, had got out three days before.

I met Mohammad Malas and Noor at a taxi rank to drive to their friend's house. The sun beat down and only when we got into the apartment elevator did Mohammad take off his cap to show me the damage inflicted by the security – a large swelling gash on the top of his skull.

We went inside the apartment – which no doubt was being monitored – and Mohammad told me the story of his detention.

"We went to the al-Hassan mosque in Midan with only pens. There were nineteen of us detained – ten guys and nine girls. Others were on their way but were stopped by the security," he said. He looked much younger than his twenty-eight years.

He and Ahmad were, in late July, invited to perform in France by the French ambassador after the diplomat saw a previous performance of theirs in Damascus. Jokingly, I asked him if he wouldn't have liked to escape it all and stay in France. "Of course not, we've got unfinished business to do here in Syria," he said with a laugh.

He was in a jovial mood as he began to tell me what happened on 13 July and during is detention.

"We believe that we are [the] artists' face to this revolution. So, when we got to the mosque some security men came straight up to us and asked what we were doing. We said we wanted freedom. He asked what did this mean. A few minutes later two buses of pro-Assad supporters arrived – they were so quick – and started shouting things in support of the president. There were only nineteen of us by that time, we were easily outnumbered. The security continued to ask us questions, they began asking to see the permission we had taken in order to hold the protest. We had none but I told him that they [the pro-Assad demonstrators] didn't have one either. 'Why don't you go ask them where their permission is,' I told the security officer. Then they started shouting saying we were spies for America and Israel, that we were not true Syrians and I was hit straight down on top of my head. There was blood everywhere. We were all handcuffed and beaten by the security. They had batons. They then kicked me up and stuffed me into a bus along with the others. At this point blood was spilling down my face and onto my clothes. They drove us to a nearby security building in Bab Musalla [a five-minute drive from where they demonstrated] and we were put in the basement. The cell was about two metres by two metres and there were ten of us. It was a horrible experience. Cockroaches crawled over our faces at night.

"The same day they took me to the hospital in Meshtahet [also close by] to get my head sewn up. The doctor was kind; he tried to take his time treating me so that I would have more time out of the cell. The security officer with me told the doctor I was fighting with other protesters and that we hit each other."

"The first day they questioned me for about forty-five minutes. They wanted to know who organised the Facebook page that called for artists and writers to gather in protest against the heavy-handedness of the regime. I said I didn't know. They even tried to convince me out of my ideas," Mohammad said with an impromptu laugh.

"On the third day, a Friday, a guy called me out and began to lecture me. 'Do you know that in Belgium they can only buy watermelons in slices, but in Syria you can buy a whole one? Do you know how expensive bread is in Lebanon or that in Argentina you can't walk in the streets after dark because it is too dangerous?'

"'What more freedom do you want than the protection Bashar al-Assad is giving you?' the guard asked me."

Though for Mohammad and the others their detention experience appeared coloured with humour, he said that the facility to which they were taken was "five star" compared to others he had heard about. "One protestor said that he had been there for fifty days. Some of the guys there had torn up tiles from the floor and cut themselves on their faces and legs so that they could be taken to hospital. They just wanted to get out.

"You could tell the time by what happened. For example, we ate at 4 and 11 o'clock, we were allowed to the toilet at 1 o'clock.

"They also brought in the men who were arrested for attacking the American and French embassies [on 11 July] but they sat drinking *mette* with the guards. They were from the same side."

He took a phonecall – to organise money for his trip to France the next day – before continuing:

"My main demand is for an end to the security state. I want the security forces gone. I follow the will of the people and if the majority want the president to stay, then that will be my will too. But I don't think he can stay. There has been too much blood and damage."

Then Eiad arrived home from his magazine's office. His eighteen-month-old daughter had just woken up. She looked happy to see me, before knocking over an empty glass next to my foot, causing much consternation in the household. Eiad sat down to talk to me but was warned by Ola not to smoke.

"I told them that I organised the protest and they beat me for that. When the others saw what was happening to me they all shouted that they organised it!"

Eiad told me he thought the regime would fall during the holy month of Ramadan, which was to begin only ten days later.

Again I asked if the country would fall into civil war should this happen.

"Syria is not like Lebanon; there they have dozens of different sects and religions. Syria has been a country for longer than the Assads – Syria is made up of people not the Assad family and its friends," he said, echoing his wife's sentiments.

***

The Local Coordinating Committees (LCC) were arguably one of the most important protest elements of the Syrian uprising. They claimed to have networked activists in the remotest of towns. They knew what was happening inside areas under lockdown for days. They could report figures of dead and injured from districts where electricity, water, internet and physical access had been denied. They were the first people to contact when a journalist needed information on events in far-thrown areas of the country.

Largely through a nerve-centre-cum-apartment in downtown Beirut, LCC members would fire out figures, videos and tweets while queuing up Skype chats with news organisations from the four corners of the globe.

Via email, and after checking my authenticity as a journalist, a member of the committees told me how the organisation operates, what it wants and what it hopes to achieve.

The committees started by meeting a number of young people and activists on the ground, where they exchanged news and ideas about the protests and how to mobilise and support protests in the other areas. The gatherings were completely spontaneous and unplanned, said the representative:

> The meetings continued this way until the situation in Deraa got worse, which made the youths realise the necessity of mobilising protests in other areas to relieve the besieged areas which are subject to maltreatment. This has motivated them to create a framework of coordination between them for that goal, and with time, the idea developed more to cover different aspects of organisation. As representatives of other areas joined, the young people decided to create committees and start a Facebook page representing them as an umbrella for their work which was born on the ground, and a hub for the news arriving from their areas.

The spokesperson said that the LCCs were "founded in Syria, but recently people from overseas joined the LCC. The LCC spreads from Deraa in the south to Idlib in the north, from coastal Banias to Qamishli in the east and to Bokamal in the desert. We have about sixteen committees [by July 2011] all over the country and are still growing".

Not all the committees received funding from people either in Syria or overseas, I was told. Members, he said, and indeed protesters who took to the streets, represented varying ages and generations.

"It's a coalition that represents the streets and in the streets there are people of all ages. What's special about the Syrian revolution, what makes it unique and different than the other Arabs revolutions is that the son is protesting with his dad and the grandfather is protesting with his grandchildren. Everyone is taking to the street to fight for their freedom."

I asked if the LCC felt responsible for the deaths of young people by calling on them to take to the streets in protest.

"We feel sorry for the loss of every person; we are losing close friends, family members and people close to our hearts. This is a revolution and we know that freedom has a high price and it's costing us our lives. We are not calling people to take to the streets – they believe that they have the right to live in a free country that should respect them and respect their rights. That's why they are taking to the streets – nothing more or nothing less."

The LCC says that the ultimate goal of the group is to "have a free country that respects us and allows us to live in dignity and respect every single right of the human being".

I asked the spokesperson if the LCC would feel responsible should civil war unfold across the country, but was told "We will never allow this to happen and so far people proved that in so many cities where the regime tried to create conflict between two different sects and failed. The civil war is a rumour the regime uses to scare Syrians and it will never happen for so many reasons, Syria is made of many sects and people with different backgrounds and beliefs and we've been living with each other for decades. We never felt our differences because we believe that we all are Syrian and that's what matter." [sic]

It was obvious that there was an ongoing blame game taking place between the activists and the regime. The activists were neither a golden salvation nor the antithesis to the Assad regime. The regime, clearly, was offering stability through its show of strength.

During the first four months the regime mixed promises of reform with deadly crackdowns. President Assad's speech to his new cabinet on 16 April was, at the time, a hugely important moment. He spoke of how:

> The more we distance ourselves from the Syrian population, the weaker our strength ... Obviously the economy is the biggest problem, and the daily needs are the greatest for the citizen who needs services, security and dignity ... I think that lifting the state of emergency will enhance security in Syria ... People want justice, they want roads, water, development, health care, education, and many other things ... There is no doubt that unemployment is the biggest problem we face in Syria ... The more transparent we are, the more we protect ourselves against unfounded allegations and charges ... The more we broaden participation, the less errors we make and the more people defend this government's decision. And the government needs people to defend its decisions.

And, perhaps the most interesting quote from that speech, "We are here to serve our citizens; and without this service there is no justification for the existence of any one of us."

These comments from the president that day showed Syrians a side of Assad many had been longing to see during those early days of unrest. Here was a man apparently in touch with his people, aware of the mistakes his government had made, keen to address the will of the Syrian population.

Reporting for *The Sunday Times*, I called up a number of Syrian friends and colleagues to see what they thought of the address.

One analyst said with an undeniable positivity how these words were what the country needed to hear. Two other twenty-something men from contrasting social and economic backgrounds were also happy with what the president said. A sense of relief and happiness was palpable in their voices when they spoke to me minutes after Assad finished his speech. The country had heard the words it had been craving for months. Millions of Syrians wanted the president to stay and to succeed. But while there was some relief on the street, protest organisers and opposition elements swiftly cast aside the speech, saying they wanted to see actions, not words. In retrospect, they were right.

***

The government lied about economic growth.

According to a 13 July post on Syriacomment, a popular blog on Syrian affairs which in turn quoted the popular SyriaNews website, Farouq al-Sharaa, Syria's vice-president, declared that Syria's growth rate never reached 6% as claimed by previous governments. These figures were "manipulated", he said, and growth never exceeded 3.7%.

Other evidence of economic troubles surfaced.

"Banks [had] to pay close to 3% higher interest rates on deposits," said the Syriacomment article. "The government is doing everything they can to support the SYP [Syrian pound] exchange rate. In the past, the Central bank intervened by selling dollars and buying SYP to try and bring the value back. They seem to have decided not to use their reserves anymore. Their plan B has just been executed. By raising rates so sharply, they hope to bring people's money back in SYP. The deposit rate now will be up to 10%. They also raised deposit rates on dollars by close to 2.5%. Unless the banks are able to raise their lending rates by as much, their profits will be wiped out. The lending rates were already close to 10%. They will have to now raise it close to 12% or higher to make any money. This is a dramatic development that will send shivers through the spine of the banking industry. Banks are being asked to subsidize the effort to stabilize the currency." [sic]

In August 2011 the Central Bank of Syria told "all banks and exchange institutions who deal with the foreign currency not to sell foreign currency except for an economic justification". Those who needed to travel overseas and, as a result, needed to buy foreign currencies, could only do so twice a year and one day before the date of travel. I visited one such currency exchange office in late July with a Syrian friend. I was told that I could not buy foreign currency. On asking if he could buy it on my behalf, my friend was told to bring a visa for the destination of travel, the plane ticket with his name on it and that he would have to be Syrian.

A Christian man I knew who had returned to Syria from the US to be married told me of his interest in buying property in Dummar, but said he wanted to wait until calm returned to the country. He had inherited over US$1.4 million and the state's interest rates convinced him to place his money in a Syrian bank. He said, in June 2011, that he would receive 10 per cent annual interest on the amount and that he couldn't turn down the offer. He would receive over 6 million Syrian pounds after twelve months simply for keeping his money in Syrian banks. He did not appear worried by the prospect of a collapse of the banking sector or in currency exchanges.

Then, in July, reports emerged that Iran was to loan Syria US$5.8 billion for economic development as well as 290,000 barrels of oil per day for one month from 13 July.

Employees of the Central Bank of Syria told me in early July that the Ministry for Finance was considering lowering the retirement age for public sector employees to fifty-two in an attempt to open up positions for young people.

The rumour, however, set off alarm bells among public workers, the bank employees said, who feared their positions would come under threat from new entry-level workers. The government's idea was to appease the country's youth but by making such an announcement it further alarmed its current employees. In a conversation with a group of public sector workers in June 2011, I told them of one experience I had in dealing with the Ministry for the Interior several months earlier.

"I was looking to get some documentation processed at the Ministry but was told it would take two months to do so," I said. "I only had a month before I needed the documents. The man I was speaking to, who worked at a small office outside the Ministry building, then asked me to meet him outside. He told me that for 30,000 Syrian pounds [about US$630] he could get the documents for me within a month. He would take care of my application personally and would use his own identification in order to sidestep the security checks. I thought it was wrong but as I needed the documents I agreed to come the following day with the money. Later I spoke to some friends who said that this amount of money was outrageous and so I didn't return to the Ministry official and made the application as normal."

I told them that this kind of corruption should be legalised.

"In Ireland if you need documents from the government in a hurry, you pay extra. You have a choice – if you don't want to pay, you wait. If you can't wait, you pay." Think of DHL, I said. "They charge a lot of money but they are offering a swift service – why doesn't the Syrian government do this?"

I told them of how I had been to the immigration and passport office over a dozen times and had only paid for stamps and official papers. "The employees – all dressed in police uniforms – got nothing for the work they did for me. If you need any process in Europe that involves the state sector you pay a charge – why don't they do the same here? Why don't they put a sign up saying 'if you need this document within one month you must pay 30,000 Syrian pounds'? Standardise the corruption; make it legal. It will bring money for the state and it will root out this culture of bribes and what essentially are informal taxes."

***

At the end of July and shortly before Ramadan began I took a trip to the Jordanian capital, Amman. The wind was so hot driving down through the black-stoned Houran region that we had to close the windows of the taxi.

Five days later, on the eve of Ramadan, 150 more people would die in a single day in Homs.

On the way to the bus station I saw five army trucks brimming with soldiers chanting support for President Assad. I shared a taxi from the Soumarieh station south west of the capital with another man, about 5" 7' and unshaven. He asked the driver to let him know if there would be any problem with his passport since the driver was obliged to record our destinations with the police at the departure office. He looked uneasy. He took great interest in several checkpoints and army installations on our journey south, though from a distance. When we got closer to the soldiers we passed before the border crossing he looked straight ahead. Passing a road entrance to Deraa, we sighted a checkpoint manned by soldiers and supported by two tanks. At this stage the man lifted himself out of his seat and strained his neck to get a better view of Deraa. Though he was entirely silent, and probably because of this, I felt something was up.

We got through the Syrian side of the border at around four in the afternoon. Our driver, who was Jordanian (something that was essential in facilitating our subsequent conversations), wanted to stop at the duty free and when he did so, Abdulrahman, the wary passenger, opened up.

His piercing blue eyes were intent as he asked me if I could put video clips up on the internet and "send them to Europe and America". At this point we were not yet technically in Jordan, on safe ground. So I said, "We'll talk in a while."

There was not an exchange of words again until after I had my passport stamped by the Jordanian authorities. The border guards went through all baggage in the car with a fine-tooth comb. They found a half-opened carton of Winston cigarettes hidden behind the plastic shell inside the boot of the car. The Assad portraits that were so plentiful in Syria and which I had not noticed for months, even years, were replaced with new faces – faces I was immediately drawn to. King Abdullah, his father, Hussein, and the young Crown Prince and heir-in-waiting, Prince Hussein, appeared in place of the Assads.

I felt a sudden wave of disappointment come over me. I had expected to breathe easy upon exiting Syria, to have a psychological weight lifted from my shoulders, to be able to say whatever I felt like after months of pressure working as a journalist inside Syria. But staring back at me from the walls of the visa offices were more strong men, more paraphernalia, more, as I felt it then, repression. I was bitterly disappointed. I felt empty.

Abdulrahman was a car mechanic from Jobar, a northern suburb of Damascus close to Harasta and Arbeen. The videos, he said, were of people being killed by the government.

Early on in the uprising he had been among the people who tried to march from Jobar to Abbasiyeen Square and who called on people to come down from their houses to join in.

Was he not afraid?, I asked him – maybe I was from the *mukhabarat*. Maybe I would report what he had said when I got back to Syria. He said that he held no fear any more.

Abdulrahman said he was in Jordan for "a day or two" to do "something". Again he said he had videos he wanted to give to me to show Europe and America.

I told him I was a journalist and had been living in Syria for several years.

"You're a journalist? Then why are you not doing anything?!" was his immediate reaction. He was totally incredulous. He simply couldn't believe there were foreign journalists in Syria at the time.

I told him it was extremely difficult to operate and that the smallest thing would see a journalist detained and/or deported from the country.

He asked me what people in other countries, in the West, thought of what was happening in Syria.

I didn't exactly know, I said, as I hadn't been in Europe for over a year, but people there knew the Syrian government was killing people for protesting in the streets. I argued that for observers outside the country the threat of civil war appeared to be growing.

He told me that one of his best friends had been shot dead by a sniper ten days previously when protesting in the streets of Jobar. As we drove south through the parched and empty Jordanian desert, Abdulrahman pulled out his phone.

On the screen of his phone I could see a thin, black-haired man, probably in his twenties, being hauled around a street by a group of people. There was a small spot of red on his left shoulder. The camera shook and after a minute or so, the man – a lifeless body – was laid on the ground. A pool of red quickly formed on the ground around his head. Men were screaming: "God is greatest. What have they done?"

This was his friend, he told me. The driver watched it too as we cruised along at 130 kilometres per hour. Another video followed, this one from Jisr al-Shaghour, he said. In this one, piles of bodies dressed in army fatigues lay in unnatural positions. I asked him where he had got it and how he knew it was from Jisr al-Shaghour. A friend gave it to him, he said. But how did he know it was real? He shrugged his shoulders and said: "The government dressed up these people in army uniform after they killed them – they're civilians. There were no weapons in Jisr al-Shaghour."

He didn't mind if another Alawite became president – democratically-elected or not – as long as the Assads were out. He said he would not rest until they were gone.

I asked him about the sectarian issue – the possibility that if protestors got what they wanted then the country would fall apart with Christians, Alawites and other minorities remaining with the government and the rest fighting against them.

"The government is pushing this religious issue to make people afraid. Do not be fooled."

Abdulrahman turned around to face me in the car twice more to make it clear that there was no religious issue within the protest movement. He said that, on Fridays, people came from the churches in Bab Touma to Jobar, a distance of a couple of kilometres, to protest against the government.

I asked when he thought the regime would fall. At the time the word on the street was that the holy month of Ramadan would make or break the protest movement – every day would become Friday. "No one knows, only God," he said, as he looked up. I asked him again.

"I am serious," he says. "Only God knows."

He gets out of the taxi, his blue eyes still aflame. Amman is dirty and appears far more religiously observant than Syria, at least anecdotally.

Living in Damascus, where on the surface life continued much as normal, one might construe sharing a taxi with a protester as pure chance. But it was something of a wake-up call for me. Parts of the countryside were by then boiling over with anti-regime sentiment as the capital, in sickly indifference, turned the other way.

***

Aspects of democratic freedom did, however, appear in Damascus and elsewhere during the unrest: people did speak freely about 'The Situation'.

The fear of talking about sensitive topics dissipated considerably and I noted to many how we would have never been able openly to discuss security issues in public twelve months earlier. This was a cornerstone of democracy, I told my friends – to be able to say what you want and not fear retribution. Democracies don't work fully in Europe or anywhere else, I said, "but we are allowed to say when we think the government is fallacious and untrustworthy. It seems today this element of democracy has reached Syria. This is the meaning of democracy – to be able to say what you want and not be afraid of being detained by the *mukhabarat*." At a restaurant in the mountain village of Erneh, four months into the uprising, my friends nodded their heads in agreement.

The gap between state and society increased significantly during the unrest. With one hand the regime offered, in words, concessions that had never been brought to light in the history of the Baath era; with the other it was responsible for large-scale terrorism against its own people.

When the state drawled on about the rallies "in support of President Bashar al-Assad's reform effort" and when video images appeared of men being shot, bodies without heads, corpses of brutalised children and massive demonstrations of people calling for the fall of the regime, what were people to think?

And how, when reading SANA, or any of the state-run newspapers, could Syrians seriously believe stories such as "In Lattakia Governorate, the governorate's branch of al-Baath Vanguards held a festivity under the title 'Syria is fine'" (SANA, 18 June 2011), or "Artificial dilemma" (*Baladna* English, 14 July 2011).

As I drove on through heavy traffic that day in Amman, a thought came to me: the protesters will not be successful until each individual in Syria has in some way been affected by the regime's heavy hand. A friend, a brother or cousin arrested and beaten. A father disappeared or his body returned.

Like an electric charge, the protest movement moved from town to town, from disaffected family to family, from brutalised neighbourhood to neighbourhood and from rumour to reality, for so many Syrians.

As the uprising made clear, when faced with a threat, the Syrian regime retreated to the comfort of its old habits, to the 1970s and 1980s, when conservatism always prevailed. The regime could have prevented the bloodshed but it chose – it chose – not to. It could have embraced the fact that people wanted to express themselves and could have facilitated this. Instead, it turned its guns on thousands of people. The regime could have embraced the March protesters, openly admitted that it – like any government around the world – had many flaws, and conveyed this to the people. The government could have ended the emergency laws when it said it would. It could have allowed peaceful protests to take place and not to spin out of control.

It is fair to say that Syrian people are defiant – certainly judging by those I have lived with for over four years. As Abdulrahman illustrated, Syrians are proud – those who want the regime to fall could not be convinced otherwise. Those who called the protesters conspirators and Islamists were equally sure in their belief that the Assad government had to stay – for whatever reasons. As the uprising wore on and as these people became further entrenched in their respective beliefs, one idea – regularly talked about over the summer of 2011 – came to reality in a sickening, self-fulfilling way: civil war.

V

REVOLUTION THROUGH THE EYES OF THE RICH AND POOR

A tale often retold by students of Arabic, tourists or visitors with a political interest in Syria is that "every taxi driver is an informer; they all work for the *mukhabarat."*

When I took the microbus into Damascus from my home – a thirty minute drive – the road was peppered with symbols and reminders that the state and its security services are never far from sight, and consciousness. The flat yellow ground that gives way to a series of hills leading south west to the Golan Heights is sectioned off by razor wire. Soldiers peer out onto the highway, their faces barely visible under large, metal helmets and bayonet-readied rifles. On the southern side of the highway is a military airfield and adjacent security compound. This is Syrian land, but it is completely off limits to Syrians.

In the first few months of the uprising, a security installation between the Mezzah highway and the Soumarieh bus terminal on the same stretch of highway would see civilian cars parked outside the compound every Thursday evening and Friday morning. The drivers of the cars were not inside for tea and a smoke, they were there planning what to do several hours later, when protestors would pour out of mosques calling for change.

As the summer wore on, the dozens of cars appeared not weekly, but daily. About a quarter of the cars were the unmistakable yellow taxis. I asked myself what taxis have to do with security. The penny soon dropped.

On the same stretch of road, though further out of the city, between the towns of Madamiyeh and Jdaydieh Artouz, a *masakin shurtah* (police housing project) was located next to the highway. These housing projects are to be found right around the country and usually consist of about a dozen poorly kept four-storey buildings. When the unrest began, the entrances were manned by armed soldiers and a lever check point. Parked inside were dozens of the ubiquitous yellow taxi cars.

So the fear of speaking about politics when taking a taxi was not unique to my own experiences but was the same for every Syrian. Sometimes taxi drivers would initiate conversations: "Oh God, save Syria," or when a BMW military-registered car sped through the street, "Who do these people think they are?" Perhaps they were checking me out, angling to see if I was 'with' or 'against' the regime. Perhaps they were genuine.

For example, when taking a taxi on the return leg from the Jordanian capital Amman to Damascus in late August 2011, as Ramadan came to a close, I asked my driver why he bought petrol from the last station in Jordan instead of waiting to pass into Syria, where fuel is considerably cheaper.

"There isn't one clean petrol station in all of Syria," boomed the taxi driver, who said he was from nearby Deraa.

What is the relationship between taxi drivers, the police and the regime's security establishments?

The answer lies in both the economic status of the average taxi driver and the fact that Syria's police are so badly paid: many policemen worked as taxi drivers, and many taxi drivers sought to add to their miserly income by informing for the security. Web was built upon web, a system the security apparatus had used for decades.

But for many even taking taxis, cheap by international standards, was unaffordable. Instead, using the omnipresent microbuses that ferried millions into Damascus each morning and home again in the afternoon was the only means of transport. State employees, up at 6am to prepare their children for school, would have breakfast and not eat again until they got home in the late afternoon via a fleet of decrepit state-owned buses. Journey after journey saw them waste away their evenings in hot, smoke-filled buses. Some that I spoke to spent ninety minutes on a bus when the direct route home took no more than twenty minutes. Still, it was provided by the state and was free. There were no mid-week restaurant trips, not even a lunch break for most in Syria's massive public sector. Just the grind of everyday life, with little prospect for a brighter future.

The gap between poor and rich in Syria was reflected most markedly during the uprising by the actions of the former and inaction of the latter. Over the decades, the countryside had been left to rot by the Baathist regime – whose original base had been there.

Hafez al-Assad seized power in 1970 and in the early years introduced projects to modernise infrastructure and brought education to the poor and to rural communities. Agrarian reforms begun by his predecessors had transformed the countryside: however, the Sunni Muslim majority in places like Hama and Homs still deeply resents the loss of vast landholdings.

But such efforts soon stopped when leading regime figures and families moved from their mountain villages to the capital. Forty years on, the Syrian countryside remains poor and isolated, with even the Alawite villages of Sheikh Badr, Ein al-Tineh, Mazar al-Qatriyeh and countless others cut off and forgotten by their sons, now driving expensive cars and night-clubbing in Damascus.

The United Nations Development Programme's study *Poverty in Syria 1996–2004* is the most comprehensive statistical report currently available. It found that the wealth gap widened and that 11.4 per cent of people, or 2.2 million of Syria's 21 million population, lived in extreme poverty, defined as unable to obtain their basic food and non-food needs, a sum equal to SYP92 or US$2 per capita per day.

When I visited the rural town of Salamieh in central Syria located close to the town of Rastan, and the cities of Homs and Hama, in 2010, there were no fancy cars but there was a tremendous peace in the spring air.

I went there with a photographer for an article about a drip irrigation project being developed by the Aga Khan Foundation that saw crops use 90 per cent of the water provided. Farming families told me how they used to harvest cotton but that now it was illegal as it used up too much water.

A shepherd boy, maybe fifteen, spent his days with a dog and about forty goats and sheep. He threw stones at the flock to stop them from eating the wrong crops. He did not go to school. His teeth were yellow and broken. Nearby, a cab-less tractor was borrowed to plough a small area to prepare it for the planting of broad beans. Thaher, the forty-something farmer of the land, said his biggest fear was frost in the coming weeks. Little did he think then that, twelve months later, detentions and shootings of locals would bear heaviest on his mind.

The flatlands around Salamieh saw havoc visit their fields outside Rastan and Talbese in 2011. A village of about 40,000 people, Rastan was subjected to numerous military operations and there were claims that the Syrian army used helicopters to launch attacks against first, demonstrating residents and later, defecting soldiers.

As was the case in the towns in Deraa province, friends told me of residents fleeing across fields, walking tens of kilometres to avoid the military and state-sponsored militias. The town of Rastan, the original home of the Free Syria Army, a loose group of defected soldiers numbering in the hundreds, is just twenty-eight kilometres from Salamieh. In late September 2011, Syrian forces entered Rastan and for three days laid waste to the rebellious town. Thousands were rounded up and put in prison. Much of the town was destroyed. Over thirty people were killed. Once more, the regime claimed victory over the 'armed gangs'. Yet the people would not lie down: by October 2011 Syrian army vehicles and posts were targeted as the Free Syria Army fought back with roadside bombs and rocket attacks from Idlib in the north to Deraa in the south. The seeds of a civil conflict were being sown.

***

Poverty was not the exclusive tenure of the rural.

In Hajar Aswad, a Palestinian camp south east of Damascus, thousands live in squalor, though of a more acute kind. They have no fields or orchards from which to fill their bellies. They must live on hard cash.

Whole families live in two-room apartments of not more than fifty square metres. A curtain is pulled over a kitchen area masquerading as another room. Pots and pans are bent out of shape from use. One woman I know whose husband was 'martyred' a few years back in Occupied Palestine raises her children on money given from a Palestinian faction.

Outside on the streets dust rises as cars speed past small children. Buildings are crammed together so closely that the air is thin and dust-laden.

At the end of a huge, fly-infested food market in Yarmouk is a roof-top Palestinian cultural centre run by a former militant turned musician. I gave classes in journalism writing there in the summer of 2010. On one occasion a woman collapsed as she stood up at the end of one of the classes. She came round a few minutes later and said she hadn't eaten all day and that most days she ate little. Once a day the director, who preaches understanding and responsibility to the dozens of unemployed Palestinians that turn up, would get someone to fetch bread, hummus and fava beans for all to eat.

The descendants of the Palestinians who fled their homeland for Syria in 1948 and 1967 today say they are Palestinian. In theory, Syria's Palestinian refugee population are still guests of the nation. However, in almost every facet of life, they are Syrian. In practice they have married into Syrian families, are allowed to own property and may attend university and work as Syrians do. Their everyday accents are Syrian.

Though it was largely ignored by the English-language media, dozens of people were killed during protests over the summer months of 2011. The area of Hajar Aswad, south east of the capital, saw dozens of anti-government protests take place with maybe two dozen deaths in May and June. Some Palestinians were protesting in support of their Syrian brothers, and against the killing of peaceful demonstrators, though the majority of the demonstrators were Syrians from the Golan Heights who had been displaced in previous wars. (They were protesting because the regime had done nothing for them since they were forced from their land. Now they lived in filth inside a Palestinian camp.) Palestinians too were shot down.

In July I had an argument with a well-educated Palestinian man in his mid-forties. "The president needs some time; you cannot expect him to change everything within a few weeks, or even months," I said.

"He is the president of the Syrian Arab Republic," he said, as he held out his arms. "If he cannot control things then what is he doing? He says changing the constitution takes time? In 2000 the constitution was changed overnight, and for what reason? To lower the age of the Syrian president from forty to thirty-six. Why? To allow him to become president. So don't tell me things take time. When they want to change things, they can do it. Don't be fooled."

Salma, not her real name, was a twenty-four-year-old Shia Ismaili woman studying for a Master's in dentistry at Damascus University, but seemed set for life as a political activist.

She met me at her clinic (many graduate students open clinics to establish themselves) in Tadamoun, close to the Palestinian Yarmouk camp, the day Gilad Shalit was exchanged for 1,027 Palestinian prisoners in October. There were major celebrations the same evening in the camp for the sixteen prisoners (according to SANA) that were sent back to Syria as part of the exchange deal.

I waited on the street outside a fast food restaurant, attempting not to appear too conspicuous. Cars flashed by on the dark streets. Lighting here was poor. Five minutes later Salma arrived wearing a broad smile. I did not return the greeting; fearful eyes were watching from the gritty shops and stalls around us – I did not want our meeting to appear overly friendly.

We crossed two streets and went down an alleyway where buildings were stacked upon each other; it was hardly possible to see the night sky above. American hip-hop blared out further down the alley and we turned into Salma's clinic. Inside, on the first floor, was Salma's assistant, who was asked to leave when we arrived. Standing on the street has made me nervous. There was plenty of time for me to have been spotted. Sean McAllister, a British journalist, was reported to have gone missing in Syria the previous day. I was thankful that the music outside in the street – now Arabic *dabke* – was loud enough to drown out our voices. At every noise from the street outside I jumped around to stare at the door.

Salma lived alone, close by. Her family lived in Salamieh, a town twenty kilometres east of Homs and Hama. She said her mother had travelled down from their home town the week before but took a road that avoided both Homs and Hama. "It's too dangerous to go near these cities," she said in a soft, English-accented voice.

Books were stacked on the desk next to her laptop. "This one is about an Iraqi man who was in prison when an American bomb landed, killing everyone but himself. So he walked alone in the desert for a long time; he had no idea the Americans had invaded Iraq or that Saddam had been defeated."

"This one, by Fouaz Haddad, a Syrian writer, is about how the state uses religion to divide people." I confirmed my suspicions; the book was published in Lebanon, not Syria.

She had started the clinic three months previously and admitted customers were hard to come by.

"I designed all of this myself, the layout, equipment, I painted the walls, this is all my own work," she sighed, with no little pride evident on her face.

The neighbourhood in which she lived and worked was run-down and working-class. She paid about US$100 a month for her apartment, but relished the independence living alone afforded her.

Salma told me her equipment was not of good quality – her dentist's chair was Chinese made: "If it was made in Italy it would last a lifetime, but I won't get that long from it."

She said she and about ten other activists met every Thursday night to discuss the situation – if, when and where they would go to protest the next day. The group usually met at one of their homes. "We don't find out where it will be held until the night before for security reasons," she said. Networking was difficult, she said, and though she did not provide information to dissidents overseas, her work was important. "I went to Antakya [in south east Turkey] when the opposition conference was held. I didn't attend the conference, it was too dangerous, but I wanted to be involved." Salma drew a series of webs on a page to explain how the activists passed information and extended their networks. "Someone I know and trust will introduce me to a new person who they trust and this is how the group grows. This is how it is being done all around the country."

Salma had not been actively anti-regime from the outset.

"I went to my first demonstration in July in Midan. It was the artists' demonstration," she said, referring to the same gathering at which Eiad Shurbaji, Ahmad Malas and Mohammad Malas were beaten and detained.

Salma told me her parents always pushed her to follow the rules in Syria; to not question the regime, to act as others do; this is a parent's way of protecting their children in Syria, she conceded. "But I've been reading since I was three years old and I know, I just know what the regime is doing is totally wrong." The fact that she, a woman, lived alone illustrated that she was clearly non-conformist.

When she went to demonstrate, usually at the al-Hassan mosque in nearby Midan, she and the women with her wore the niqab – the full-body Islamic cover – to prevent identification.

She told me she had attended the funeral of Ibrahim al-Shayban the previous Saturday. Ibrahim was fourteen years old when he was shot dead by Syrian security forces.

"There was a massive crowd at the funeral. We said prayers at the al-Hassan mosque and when we got outside we started shouting for the downfall of the regime. We walked with the family to the graveyard – there were still thousands. Most people waited outside the graveyard as the family went inside. Then a group of about 100–200 people carrying pictures of the president and shouting slogans for the regime walked towards us. They started shouting insults at us and some fights started. Then the security forces came and I ran away." One man was shot dead and five people were injured in Midan that day.

I asked if she did not think it wrong to use the Islamic scarf to conceal her intentions; she didn't normally.

"Almost all the girls put it on when they go to protest. Listen: I am no good to my country if I am locked up in a jail after being identified. I'm no help to anyone if that happens. So we do what we can, any way we can."

"OK, but when the rest of Syria – and the outside world – see women covered in conservative Islamic dress does this give the impression that this is an Islamic revolution – making Syria's minorities and the rest of the world more afraid of what might happen should the regime fall," I said. She replied that the people of Syria knew it was not an Islamic revolution.

There is a saying in Arabic about the Ismailis from Salamieh that they are 'thinkers, poor, and liberal', a friend had told me. She told me that what she saw in Salamieh was "beautiful; we have anti-regime protestors walking on one side of the street and a rally for Bashar al-Assad on the other side of the street and no one fights. This is the meaning of democracy."

She called herself the 'opposition' and said that it was normal that the minorities were fearful of change. "I am from a minority – Shia people – even the Alawites do not think of us as being Muslims at all so most Ismailis are afraid of a conservative government or society taking over if the Assad regime is toppled."

"The last thing we need is for NATO or America or Turkey to come and help us. This will destroy the country and I know that if they come it will only be for their own interests. They will come for oil, politics, power. I do not want freedom if it is free – if it is handed to me," she said, her eyes wide, her voice louder. Her suspicion of the motives of western countries was patent.

"So how many people must die for you to get what you want? Is it not wrong that people are dying every day?" I asked.

"This is the price of freedom. I don't know how long this situation will go on for but we have to do it our way."

We turned to the Free Syria Army, and whether this loose group of defected soldiers that by December 2011 had carried out a number of attacks against the Syrian army and state-owned buildings might help the opposition defeat the regime.

"A friend videoed clashes between the defectors and army troops in Homs recently. He said the army troops could barely hold the guns – they were shaking and didn't know how to use the weapons; many were shot down by the defectors. So it is clear that these soldiers are the young, uneducated, poor conscripts – none of the important soldiers or officers are risking their lives. This is why we hear of soldiers being martyred in the state news."

Salma's energy, colour and drive allowed me to hope that Syria's future would be a bright blend of life brought about through its mix of religions and sects. In a country where generations-old norms are deeply ingrained, Salma, even for her young years, was inspirational. On 17 February 2012, Salma was detained.

I walked to a street corner and waited for a microbus to take me back to the city centre. On the way bottles of Almasa and Amstel beer appeared conspicuous inside the doors of local shops. I thought how in the wealthy, supposedly liberal areas of Damascus selling alcohol was unheard of. Yet here in the slums, people lived with a sense of tolerance and liberty. There was respect for differing, often opposing values. The streets were barely paved. Outside a magnificent mosque not far from Midan, two buses – the notorious kind – were parked between rows of carpets, now on sale for the coming winter months. People wove in and around fast food joints, shops selling a plethora of nut varieties and cheap toys.

***

Perhaps the most explicit differences between rich and poor may be seen in Kafr Souseh, Damascus. Today Kafr Souseh is a home for the city's super rich, boasting apartments that fetch upwards of US$1 million; the average one-bedroomed apartment cost in 2011, on average, around US$100,000 in Damascus. But just twenty years earlier the neighbourhood was a horticultural centre; the chief source of thyme and other fresh vegetables for people in Mezzah, Baramkeh and other southern districts in the capital. Today, a number of farms still remain in the area where shoppers at the two local malls can catch glimpses of cows and calves – and the accompanying rustic smells – on their way back to their cars, Gucci bags in hand.

The Rifai mosque on Kafr Souseh square quickly became one of only two centre-points for protest inside the capital. Its chief sheikh, Osama al-Rifai, and his brother Sariya, are important leaders of the Zayd *jamiyyat*, the most popular religious trend in the capital. Since returning from exile in Saudi Arabia in 2000, they continue to attract thousands of followers. The Zayd organisation also runs charities through Damascus and elsewhere that provides food for thousands of poor families. On 1 April 2011, around 600 worshippers-turned-protestors locked themselves inside the vast white-stoned building and, in late August, the eighty-year-old Osama al-Rifai was beaten and one protestor killed by a mixture of security personnel and government thugs.

Abu Fares was a shopkeeper from the southern verges of Baramkeh. He had been trying to sell his 1970s Volkswagen Beetle for months and when I entered his shop to buy gum, juice or cigarettes, Abu Fares had Quranic verses playing from a television over his door.

Though it was clear Abu Fares was a religious man, I never thought of him as politically active until I heard in May 2011 that he had been arrested.

"Abu Fares would talk to everyone and anyone about politics, about how bad the government was, about how religion should be given more study in schools," a worker in another nearby shop told me. "He was caught after he started complaining about the regime killing and detaining people in front of a bunch of customers. One of his customers was from the *mukhabarat*." I went to his shop about a week after Abu Fares had been released. He seemed a little thinner, but carried on engaging in the same anti-regime conversations. Al Jazeera was beaming out images of protests from his television over the door.

He was one of the thousands who attend prayers at the nearby Rifai mosque each and every Friday, and one of millions of religious Sunni Muslims in Syria emasculated by the authorities, whom they see as led by the philandering, irreverent and far from pious Alawite Assads. He was also part of a smaller group of Muslims devout to the teachings of the rebellious Rifai mosque, a thorn in the side of the regime since the days of the 1979–82 Islamic rebellion.

For the poor families of Kafr Souseh, who lived on the northern and southern patches of empty space, they had to put up with the checkpoints set up outside their doors. Their meagre income from homemade milk, cheese and yoghurt they made with their own thin, Friesian cows was rarely enough, and they regularly turned to the Rifai mosque and to others in Midan for clothes and other household necessities.

***

Though well over half the Syrian population lives in the cities of Damascus, Aleppo, Homs, Lattakia and so forth, around eight million people lived in dust-laden, dilapidated villages and farms that would not have looked out of place in nineteenth-century Europe.

In the north east, once the country's wheat basket, farmers are almost totally reliant on irrigation for their livelihoods. In the countryside of Hassake, Raqqa and Deir Ez Zour farmers used open water irrigation channels made from concrete for decades. However, this system was a poor one. It was exposed to the elements and any shift or movement would see it cracked with the irrigated water seeping into the ground before it reached the crops. Millions of litres of water were wasted.

The drought of 2008–09 devastated the livelihoods of hundreds of thousands of farmers and labourers. Herders had to sell up to 80 per cent of their livestock. Some 800,000 people had their livelihoods destroyed. Around 300,000 families were forced to move to urban centres across the country. Poverty levels in some communities stood at 80 per cent.

From 2008 on, thousands of farmers moved to Deraa in search of work in importing and exporting over the Jordanian border. Others bunked down on the floors of friends' houses in suburbs of Damascus, lucky to get hold of a taxi to work for a few hours, fumbling their way around the streets of the capital during the dark hours of the night. Many took to construction work, earning about US$10 for a day of hard labour among Damascus' numerous construction sites. More still went to work for the security services, either as informers or as part of the groups of men paid to beat demonstrators in Midan and elsewhere, as part of the *shabiha*.

They lived in Harasta, Madamiyeh, Hajar Aswad and Douma – all centres for protest against the government. A Kurdish friend told me in 2009 how he rented a room in a house for 2,000 Syrian pounds (US$22) per month. He shared the house with a family from Iraq. He had hated the regime long before the 2011 uprising took place.

In March 2011, as protests began to take hold across Syria, I visited directors at the Ministry for Irrigation in the north Damascus suburb of Harasta. They were all in a great state of worry.

They complained to me that their workloads had long been unmanageable. Several of them would work from 8.30am to 3.30pm and then return to their offices from 6pm until 11pm to go through more paperwork. Plans for a new massive irrigation project using Syria's forty-four kilometre stretch of the River Tigris were being drawn up when I visited. Several days later all directors at the Ministry, the minister for irrigation as well as a number of related ministers, were summoned for a meeting in the eastern city of Deir Ez Zour. The two-day conference (of the four directors I spoke to, none of them had any interest in going all the way out into the desert, but were obliged to attend) was hastily called in order to show locals in the area – the Syrians who were in the worst need of state assistance – that the government had not forgotten them, that it was going to spend money to help the farmers. Months later, in early August, the residents of Deir Ez Zour were on the receiving end of a very different message from the regime. Thousands of troops entered the city on 7 August, following a shelling campaign at the end of July. At least fifty people were reported to have been killed in less than forty-eight hours.

Many English-language newspapers and television stations referred to Deraa, Douma, and Jisr al-Shaghour as "poor towns". The reason these areas saw renewed protests was exactly because they are poor and because the Baath party, founded in the countryside under a supposedly socialist flag, simply forgot about them. Anyone who has taken a public bus to the pre-Roman ruins in Palmyra – 'the Bride of the Desert' – will have seen the destitution locals live in. The town of Tadmor (where protests took place for months, but were not covered in media reports) sits adjacent to the ancient Temple of Baal and other breathtaking several-thousand-year-old ruins. Children in the town, cleft-lipped and visibly malnourished, sit in rags on street pavements. Young men with nothing to do, no jobs or entertainment, drive motorbikes around the town for hours. There is no industry, only a vast prison and a number of security depots. And thousands of tourists and archaeologists visit the ruins – a fifteen-minute walk from the town centre – each year. The children who walk aimlessly around the ruins at Palmyra selling postcards – though they speak a word or two of English – have no education, no health care, or no outlook for the rest of their lives except selling these postcards. The young men on camels have little or no futures to plan for. They see little beyond staring at the foreign young women that come to experience the mystical Syria ruled by the great Queen Zenobia.

***

In a sense, dissent from the poor was always coming – the only question was when. But this revolution, which started in the provinces, could only succeed by rousing the populations of the industrial and commercial heartlands: the cities of Aleppo and Damascus.

To say that the wealthy of Damascus and Aleppo didn't protest simply because they were afraid of the value of their homes decreasing or because they were afraid of the security services is simplistic. These major population centres suffered significant physical destruction during past revolts and war. The number of *Shuam* I spoke to through 2011 who were disinterested in the violence of the countryside for the initial few months, only to thereafter express outright anger at the government, increased exponentially. The business classes can roughly be divided into two groups of 'big families'. Those that preceded both the Assad regime and Baathist ideology included the Qalla, Sabbagh, Qabban and Haffar families that were never particularly supportive of the regime – they saw them as putting their hands in the merchants' pockets. The second group are referred to as the 'Children of Authority' by academic Salwa Ismail and were those who attempted to move into the business sphere following the amalgamation of business and Assad power.

These included the Nahas, Joud and Tlas families as well as those under direct Assad family patronage such as the Makhlouf, the Shalish and the Shawkat families. The 'Children of Authority' flourished in business circles that produced new products: computers, telecommunications and network logistics. These families could never have been expected to move against the regime had they nothing left but pocket change; they would never support protests.

For the revolution to be successful it had to incorporate elements in business; it needed the support of the moneyed and powerful. By September, the Syrian government had banned the importation of all goods subject to customs tax of 5 per cent or more, in a move to protect its foreign currency reserves. It was a startling decision. It illustrated once again how the regime was willing to go back to the time of Hafez al-Assad, to revert inwards, to go back to isolation, to a flawed idea of self-sustainability. Only those inside the clique of power would be able to buy cars, flat screen TVs, laptops, Italian marble and so on. It sent the business class into a major panic. Those who had made hundreds of millions importing much sought-after products, from shaving gel to perfume for the new bourgeoisie, were up in arms.

Around the same time an increase in the price of items essential to a household food basket took hold, partly because Syrians began hoarding food and other products. A pack of cigarettes went from 80 to 130SYP, a litre of milk from 45 to 55SYP and a dozen eggs from 80 to 100SYP. Petrol stations had fuel for only a few hours a day as motorists and men on foot queued up before reserves quickly ran out. Heating fuel and gas for cooking were available on the street at 200 per cent of the official price, if at all, by December. The other option was to register at a local fuel distributor and wait one month in the hope of receiving a few hundred litres. In late November, locals said heating fuel trucks in the town of Qatana had to be accompanied through the streets by armed soldiers, such was the demand, and feeling of lawlessness. Gas and *mazout* – the heating oil – became as precious and as rare as gold during a winter that was unusually early and abnormally cold.

Several days after the lifting of the import ban was officially announced (though in actuality the 'law' was not recanted for several weeks), I visited Abdul Ghani Attar, Vice-President of the Attar Group, at his offices in leafy Rowda in Damascus.

At 9am he was a little flustered. A Bachelor's degree from McGill University hung on the wall behind him. In a cabinet to his left were books by Bill Gates, Warren Buffett and other world business leaders.

A copy of the Quran sat atop a three-foot high speaker, next to a flatscreen television made by Sony, a company for which Attar holds the import licence in Syria.

Attar told me that within the first three months of the crisis economic activity fell dramatically, people were in shock. But now, as schools opened and life was returning to normal, business activity was down 40 per cent. "People are spending more on restaurants and so forth, which helps the local economy, because they are not making major purchases."

The Attar Group, established in 1922, predates the current Baathist regime by quite a distance. It runs the gorgeous Carlton Hotel next to the breathtaking Aleppo Citadel.

"Blackberry couldn't enter the Syrian economy because, as a Canadian company, it didn't want to go against America's lead in sanctioning Syria. We may see a return to the 1980s but the regime is quite resourceful, it is tougher than people think," he said.

"The sanctions are supposed to affect certain individuals but we know this will not be the case. They have had their foreign assets frozen which has put them into [a] 'we will fight to the end' mentality. They feel they are under siege. The idea is to target certain members of the regime but we know from the past that it will affect business people and Syrians in general."

Mr Attar explained how there were two tiers in the Syrian economy. The vast majority – 80 per cent – is the general market, and goods for this, such as clothes and basics, come from China and wider East Asia. The other 20 per cent, the luxury market, was clearly affected by the unrest.

"If this situation continues for three, six or even twelve months I think businesses will survive, the regime will survive. But if it continues past this it will be difficult for everybody."

Six days after the government introduced the temporary 'suspension' of all imports with over 5 per cent tax charges, I met Osama, a businessman. A yellow dust had been hanging heavy in the Syrian air all day, covering cars, newspaper stands and exposed restaurant furniture. Osama imports generators from around the world, with Turkey his largest supply source. I knew Osama but his light blue eyes had never been so angry. He was furious with the government. He wanted it to fall immediately.

"50 per cent of my business is importing generators and 50 per cent is importing spare parts for generators," he fumed.

He told me he had just signed a contract for the delivery of a cargo of generators from Turkey but had had to cancel because of the government's new import ban. "I should have paid the Turkish company two thousand dollars but they were kind enough to waive this – they know things are difficult for Syrians," he said, grimly.

All the businessmen he knew, he said, including those who operated in the free zones, were in a rage. Car imports dropped from 20,000 in March to 2,000 in May.

I told him the Christians I knew were very afraid. "Listen, there is no problem for Christians in Syria. Fares Khoury was our president once." I had clearly started Osama thinking. "Going back decades Christians have been well treated here. When a Christian neighbour of my grandfather in Midan wanted to move to Qassaa [a Christian area in Damascus] my grandfather pleaded with him to stay in the neighbourhood. He said 'don't sell your house, rent it if you want, but don't sell it – we don't want to lose you here!'"

"We had Alawite, Shia, Christian and Jewish families living on our street before the Assads came. Nobody cared about religion in those days. My grandmother died when my father was only a couple of months old. There was nowhere he could get milk. Then a Christian neighbour came over and asked my grandfather to take my father for a few days to keep him healthy, to breastfeed him.

"That's how close we used to be; and now see how things have changed!"

"I am positive for two reasons. One, that we are now able to talk about politics openly in public; people are not afraid to do this anymore. The second reason is that this regime will fall." This thought clearly gave him hope. He looked like someone definitely in need of hope.

He told me how he was among a group of businessmen who had been to see the minister of economy and trade a couple of days before to complain about these "crazy moves".

"The minister said he could do nothing. It was completely over his head."

It became clear to me that the corruption involved in business transactions had been eating away at him for years. More than three times during our conversation he returned to the issue of paying bribes to officials and employees. "I pay the official customs tax which is fine. Then I have to pay a bribe to get my products out of the port, and on to the free zone near Damascus. Then another bribe to get them out of the free zone and into the market. Only then can I begin to make money."

"You know what?" he said. "I'll just get my products shipped to Lebanon and then use the smugglers to bring them over the mountains. In the end paying the smugglers will cost me the same as the bribes!"

In a surprising U-turn, less than two weeks later the government cancelled the ban on imports. The move made it look bumbling and weak, and underlined the massive gap between the regime's thinking and the demands of the people. SANA reported that: "In an interview with the Syrian TV, Minister of Economy and Trade Mohammad Nidal al-Shaar said that the decision to suspend importation had a negative impact on the market and raised the prices of goods, and that the decision was reversed due to the legitimate demands of citizens as it had more negative repercussions than expected." [sic]

Businessmen were left scratching their heads while foreign analysts and commentators waited in hope for the business class to 'peel away' from the regime. But in fact there was little or no relationship between business leaders and the regime during the revolt. The majority were frozen by fear.

"I would love to send money to the opposition in Turkey, but I am sure there are spies; it is too risky," a businessman who imported cars told me in October 2011. The story of an unnamed businessman who went protesting in Midan early on during the revolt was doing the rounds among business leaders. He was caught and imprisoned and only managed to be released because a friend met President Assad by chance and asked for a personal favour. "There is no one in the business community who can pick up the phone and call the regime leadership," said another leading businessman whose company produced glass and aluminium. "There is no contact; they do not come to us for money in these times."

One of the most markedly visible signs of the wealth gap in Syria can be seen in restaurants, which vary considerably in prestige and quality.

Owned by the Gemini Group, Sahara restaurant on the Mezzah highway attracts the rich like few others. Here the city's wealthy and connected pass in and out in plain view of the traffic-bound masses, feet away from the outermost tables. Anyone who is anyone comes to Sahara; from the higher echelons of the *mukhabarat*, pulling up outside in their blacked-out SUVs (they do not pay), to the city's leading businessmen.

Twenty-four-year-old Rana was one of Damascus' young rich daughters. From Midan, her father sells fabric and upholstery material in the Hariqa area of the Old City, just south of Souk Hamadiyeh.

Sucking on the omnipresent *argeleh* water pipe, Rana, a Sunni, maked it clear she was hoping unreservedly for the regime to collapse. Today.

"When I was fifteen a senior officer from the security came to my family to ask to marry me. He wanted to take me to Lebanon. He was Alawite and because he had this power, he thought he could come and just take me as he liked, away from my family, away to another country," she said. At that time Syria had essentially been occupying Lebanon. "These people think they are above everyone else, that they are more than human! How dare they!"

Fouad, a Kurdish-Armenian architect, was more nuanced in his views, though no less forceful. He designed some of the country's biggest development projects and had worked for one of Syria's high-ranking soldiers.

Fouad told me that before the unrest he employed twenty people, most of whom were graphic technicians and designers. Now he had only four employees and no projects in Syria.

"Hafez al-Assad is ruling Syria today, from his grave!" exclaimed Fouad, a father of two with a small, excitable face.

"In the past Syria was part of a great country, an empire. Today we have nothing in our country."

I asked him why.

"Because of the government. They are the reason."

He took out his laptop to show me some of his past projects. The Syrian rich are not ready for today's architectural styles, he told me, so "I build what was popular in Europe forty years ago. They like this era of architecture."

Among his portfolio are malls, country villas and Oriental-styled hotels and mansions in Doha.

But he disagreed with Rana. He was of the opinion that if the regime were to fall then there would be total chaos. They need time, he said. I argued with him, saying that dozens were dying 190 kilometres up the highway in Rastan that same day. The government has failed to deliver on any of its promises, I said.

"And the people know this. They are not stupid," I added. "Why can't they just call in the military? Put the army and security services back in their bases and if there are gangs still carrying out attacks then let journalists like me go see what it is they are doing."

"Listen, the Middle East is like an arch and Syria is the key stone right in the middle of this arch. If you pull this out the whole arch collapses," he responded. "If there is war in Syria it will involve Hezbollah, and then Iran and then Israel and Saudi Arabia. We need to be very careful not to let Europe into Syria. They want to control us, to exploit us."

He said Europe should continue to pressure the government, but he seemed completely opposed to foreign intervention in Syria. "What will happen is that 22 million Syrians will unite to fight NATO or Turkey or whoever. We need to give them time, and if they [the regime] don't do anything then I will be the first to go on to the streets to protest. What people are doing now is stupid. They cannot achieve anything."

Rana curtly interjected. "Every Friday I see the security hit and shoot at people coming out of the al-Hassan mosque next to my home [in Midan]. What kind of behaviour is this? How can we allow them to stay in power when they do this?"

Fouad dismissed her statement.

"Well they should continue to hit and shoot these people. They speak of freedom but they have no idea what it means. They think it as simple as 'get rid of the Assads and our lives will be amazing'. This will not happen. There will be civil war before that happens!"

"I want my children to grow up in this country and to be educated here. But if we collapse the regime – and I am totally against the regime – then I will probably have to take my family and live in another country."

Fouad called out to a friend several tables to our left.

"How is work?" he asked.

"I need to talk to Ban Ki-moon!" his friend shouted back. Fouad informed me that his friend imported sports equipment and since the import ban, business for him too had dried up.

They went on smoking their *argelehs*.

***

Among a throng of students, still energetic having been back at university just a week, I got off a microbus outside the faculty of literature at Damascus University on the Mezzah highway.

At the main gate a young man and woman were checking bags and IDs. I had no ID, but was told by my friend inside to say I was going to the university hospital. I did so and they waved me in. Inside was Khaled (not his real name), an irrepressible Christian friend, always the heart and soul of any social gathering. His friend from Hama, a city that has suffered at the hands of the regime like no other, shook my hand. On benches around the campus friends sat chatting under a sun that had now lost its months-long ferocity. Firas (also not his real name) was studying for a PhD in dentistry. He said he had returned from Hama just that morning. We walked through the campus to a Spartan cafeteria and sat at the end of a room crowded with students, all chatting loudly about their past summer experiences.

On 2 July, the president sacked the governor of Hama province. Six days later the French and American ambassadors to Syria made an unannounced and unauthorised visit to the city. The regime saw it as foreign interference.

Firas told me that the number and frequency of army checkpoints are the reason the 500,000-strong demonstrations that took place during the summer months had now dwindled inside Hama and in the other major centre of unrest, Homs.

In Homs, a city of one million, there are two main Alawite neighbourhoods, populated by people who came from the villages and towns over the past half century to join the armed forces, and to benefit from the Assads' hold on power by getting work in the city's state institutions.

Many Christians in the city fled in the summer of 2011 because of fear of violence, though the vast majority were not forced out, as some news outlets reported.

Baba Amr, Khaladiyyeh, Karm Al-Zeitun and Wadi al-Shayeh were the main focal points for, at first, military attacks on noted protest leaders, then on defected soldiers, and finally, by December 2011, combat between battalions of the Free Syria Army and regular troops.

As defections grew, soldiers fled to neighbourhoods such as Baba Amr, taking great risks as they did so. Dozens of checkpoints were set up in this neighbourhood alone, with over 500 throughout the city of Homs. Defectors, overwhelmingly conscripts and overwhelmingly Sunni, were sheltered by sympathetic Sunnis, families who had lost fathers, brothers and sons at the hands of the regime's punishing attacks.

Soldiers were commanded to shoot protestors while the security forces stood behind them – their own guns aimed at the soldiers. "If we didn't shoot the protestors we would be shot by the security forces – we were stuck in the middle," one defected NCO told Al Jazeera in early December 2011.

There was no rubbish collection for weeks. Rats multiplied. As with the rest of the country, there were extremely low supplies of cooking gas and, heating fuel, with daily power cuts and paltry amounts of food, but in Homs supply lines were cut – at least in most other parts of the country free movement meant provisions could be borrowed from extended family or friends. In Homs this couldn't take place.

Homs city centre – where hundreds of thousands of protestors gathered during the summer at Clock Square, embracing what we know now was a false freedom, was relatively safe – the regime still held sway. It was the suburbs that saw terror and confusion – as defected troops with arms, backed by channels running guns and ammunition from Lebanon just thirty kilometres to the west, fought back against the regular army, locals were caught in the crossfire.

People were buried in public parks. Days later the government would send teams to dig up the bodies and rebury them elsewhere so as not to leave any potential for future accusations. Protests were increasingly held at night.

By December running battles between the FSA and the army/military were taking place in these neighbourhoods and in Deraa and Idlib provinces, but the situation in Syria had not reached the level of civil war.

Alawites in Homs – about 20 per cent of the city's population – sided with the regime for a simple reason: Bashar al-Assad's security and officer corps were staffed by Alawites – they were family and friends of the Alawites inside the towns and cities.

The residents of Hama told similar, though less brutal stories.

"There are less people demonstrating because as soon as the security hears people shouting they all group up and move to that area within one minute. Then the demonstrators run away," said Firas.

Aware of the historical precedent, the regime felt it could not allow Hama to remain what was essentially at that time a free city, during the entire month of Ramadan. At the time, demonstrations initiated one of the regime's most severe crackdowns.

On the morning of 31 July, it launched a vicious assault on the city. Then, in the early days of Ramadan in August, the Syrian army shelled the city centre and seized control of the main square as well as most of the city. Eighty people were reported to have died on 31 July – the day before the fasting month began – one of the deadliest days the country had seen.

Firas had opened a can of peach iced tea but it sat untouched in front of him; he was too busy talking. He told me several of his cousins died during the 1982 attack on the city. Today, he knew around twenty people who had been killed and maybe fifty who had gone missing, presumed detained or dead.

He told me that the protests had evolved because of the security and army presence around the city. "Now people protest in the Old City, where the alleyways are narrow and it is harder for the security to find demonstrators."

"If anyone walks on to the main square to demonstrate they will be shot directly," he stated, his eyes beaming.

I asked him if the sheikhs in the city's mosques encouraged people to defy the regime or the opposite. "No they are not telling people to protest – they cannot. But nor are they asking people to be quiet."

Firas said that some Alawite and Christian families moved out of the city because "they are afraid of the violence, not because they are afraid of us."

"In the beginning we had Alawites, Christians and Sunni *Hamwi* [people from Hama] demonstrating but the others [Alawites and Christians] stopped attending protests when we stopped calling for freedom and started calling for the downfall of the regime."

He also said he had seen soldiers shooting at each other in the streets below his house.

A second friend of Khaled's arrived and sat down next to me. He was dressed in pale green hospital scrubs, and was evidently keen to tell his story.

Hani was from the town of Souran, eight kilometres north of Hama. I had wanted to meet him as he was from an area suffering the wrath of the regime at the time, but also because Khaled had told me of his conservative views.

"What kind of Syria would you like to have?" I asked Hani. "One that is free, one that has democratic elections. I think 70 per cent of the people are Islamic and that they would vote for an Islamic government," he said.

A few minutes later Firas announced he had to leave. He stood up and said in a low but forceful tone: "We want freedom!" in broken English.

I asked Hani if he thought Syria would become more Islamic if the regime were to fall.

"Today we have girls wearing short sleeves and short dresses. This is not right. The regime has allowed these things to happen and Syria is an Islamic country – it is wrong to have this. It is not right to have a man and woman walking in the streets together if they are not married. Other people see this and then they think it is OK and that it is normal. This is not right."

"But if someone wants to go to a pub or casino then that's his business; he should be allowed do what he wants, right?" I asked Hani.

"Yes, but when people see these things in front of them they are drawn or are seduced into going to such places. On TV we have stories of men and women cheating and lying. These shows put bad ideas into people's heads."

Khaled, the Christian, told me later how Hani told him a story about his friends in Souran who attacked a military building and smashed an officer's head in with a stone. "He boasted about this story when he told me. What the hell? This is crazy!"

The meeting ended like most in which I have partaken – with the Syrians joking that they hoped I was not a spy. I always thought the reverse – that these guys could have been setting me up.

VI

THE UPRISING AND SYRIA'S YOUTH

According to a 2010 European Union report, a massive 70 per cent of Syria's population is under thirty years old. The labour force will continue to expand by 250,000 to 300,000 individuals every year for the next twenty years. If the Syrian government didn't face a problem with the country's youth in the past, it certainly does now.

In Egypt and elsewhere across the Middle East and North Africa, the youth played a pivotal role in ousting dictatorial governments by demanding change and a better life.

In Syria the situation was no different.

Some sided with the government; some hopefully awaited its downfall, while others took up activist work. Many bled, were tortured and were killed for freedom. All believed the status quo had come to an end. A protest movement that began in the countryside and was, for months, ignored by the young city elite was met with severe challenges. To start with, those in the villages and towns were not, for the most part, well-connected to the outside world, and hence, word of the protest movement faced difficulties in reaching a wider audience. The wealthy, those who spent hours online every day, did not want change – they were happy with what they had; they had no need for liberty.

In Damascus, the vast majority of young people go to university, and have done so for decades as a result of the socialist approach to education that has largely pervaded since the 1960s. A few with enough money or who enjoy good relations with their lecturers go on to pursue graduate studies. The buildings of the state universities are all ugly, hulking masses of sun-beaten concrete constructed decades ago. Inside the Faculty of Law at Damascus University, for example, is a courtyard where couples sit on broken benches. Grass and weeds clamber up through the cracked paving. The fountain – perhaps once the yard's centre-piece – is dry. Inside one building corridor, students jump over water puddles on the floor. The classrooms are large and empty except for the broken blackboards and long, twisted benches where students sit and listen to their professors lecture. There is no air conditioning for the summer and in winter the heaters are empty.

What student could gain inspiration or motivation in such an environment I wondered, when watching President Assad's tel-evised speech from Damascus University on 20 June, if he had seen what I had. Of course he hadn't.

As in many so-called developed countries, having a univer-sity or graduate degree does not guarantee work in Syria. What it does guarantee is social acceptance among one's peers and family which, at least, is a start for any young man or woman setting out to carve a path for themselves in this most rigid of societies.

Fields like IT and computing hold a natural attraction for young people and a flourishing number of computer shops in and around Damascus provide part-time employment and a bet-ter understanding of the outside world to many, but, conflicting with Syrian society, these fields are not compatible with a sta-ble long-term future and marriage prospects. Young doctors and dentists, though highly prized for social status reasons, rarely make more than enough to get by.

In Syria, the issue is not so much unemployment as underem-ployment, a common complaint in a plethora of former commu-nist and socialist countries during the twentieth century.

A 2011 report by Nader Kabbani, then the head of research at the Syria Trust for Development, found that there needed to be a move "beyond knowledge transfer to skill development" as well as "more low/medium skilled jobs ... to absorb displaced agricultural workers".

A 2008 article published in *Gulf News* and written by Sami Moubayed, who taught Syrian history at the University of Kalamoon, reported that "young Syrians were more impressed by a leader who could attract investment, create jobs and build a success story for his country from scratch ... than one who preached revolutionary socialism and promised to defeat the State of Israel." It was a sly pointer to President Assad.

Thousands of youthful Syrian men leave for the Gulf in search of work every year, and to escape the dreaded mandatory military service. In 2008 military service, in which every able Syrian man must partake (unless he has no brothers), stood at two years. In part because of the unrest, compulsory military service was reduced to eighteen months in 2011. This long-term hole in their lives has led young men to depart Syria in the thousands, increasing the effects of brain drain. The government has responded, to an extent, by introducing laws that allow men to avoid military service if they stay overseas for five years (they are allowed to return home one month per year) and pay around US$5,000 to the state. If they do not, these men can expect to be arrested and forcibly led into the army, as happened to one Damascene man I know in 2010.

Damascus' teenagers, the generation that may well be responsible for the critical first steps of a new Syria, are defying the age-old rules expected from and applied by their families.

Men are waiting longer to get married in order to further their careers and to evolve their own individual identities.

The unbending force of western languages (predominantly French and English), culture and social norms are growing by the day through satellite television and cheap copies of Hollywood films.

Cross-dressers and transvestites are seen regularly on the streets of Shaalan and Malki in Damascus' more liberal areas. Emo youths sporting straightened and dyed long hair and eyeliner in the same areas of the city are a common sight day or night.

The boys of Damascus are more treasured by their parents than their high-maintenance sisters. With the girls there is more at risk – the entire family status is on the line if a daughter is, for example, seen with a boy alone to whom she is not a) related, b) engaged or c) married. She is practically worthless if she gains a 'reputation', a word with frighteningly significant social capital. If she ever became pregnant the entire family name would be destroyed. The girl would in all likelihood be forced to marry the person she copulated with. In four years of living in Syria I have never heard of an unmarried girl getting pregnant, but of course it happens.

And there are countless other social pressures on Syria's youth today.

A friend, Samir, once told me of his friend's predicament.

The friend wanted to marry a girl from a family that was not well-to-do, but not poor.

As is customary, the man went to the girl's house to ask her parents for their daughter's hand in marriage. He sat down with the girl's father.

"Do you have a house?" asked the father.

"Yes, I have, in Qudsayieh suburb," he said, referring to an up-and-coming area west of Damascus where property remains relatively inexpensive.

"We were thinking about a house in Rowda," replied the father, referring to a beautiful neighbourhood in central Damascus where trees shade French colonial-era houses and properties sell for tens of millions of Syrian pounds.

"Do you have a car?" asked the father.

"Yes, a Kia," replied the boy.

"We were thinking about an Audi or Volkswagen or something like that," said the father, again disappointed.

Samir told me the girl's father would not bless the engagement because he had other ideas for his daughter. The couple was devastated. There was no marriage.

***

In June of the year of the uprising, I sat down with a friend at a café popular with young people in Rowda in the heart of the capital, days before he travelled to Spain to continue his dentistry studies. He wanted to buy some property for his family, and feared the growing unrest and the economic consequences it carried. I wanted to know what he thought, as a twenty-eight-year-old Damascene, of the difficulties facing the country's youth and how he planned to get through what was formerly 'The Situation' but at that point 'The Crisis'.

The first issue he brought up, was religion.

"We all know Christians and we are respectful of them, as they are with us. But we never delve deep into each other's religious lives; we never talk about religion or the things that make us different from each other," he said.

According to him, the uprising and protests had happened in towns and villages closed off from religions that were not theirs. "The people who are taking to the streets and calling for the end of Bashar don't realise the consequences of this. People will go out and slaughter each other because one is not a Sunni or Shia or Alawite or Christian."

I told him I knew a Christian population in a town outside Damascus well and that they frequently made disparaging comments about Muslims. I told him they all lived in one small area of the town, grouped together in a bubble, and wrapped up in each others' lives, and that there had been anti-government protests in this town. They bought clothes from Christian-owned shops; they brought in a Christian guy to fix their television cables. The local convenience store was owned by a Christian. They would drive to the opposite side of Damascus – over an hour's journey – to open a bank account because they knew a Christian man working there.

"So don't tell me that the protests are only taking place in areas where there is a single religion," I told him.

"People in towns and cities who live with Christians, Alawites, Shia and so on know each other. They know there is a difference but they never address this," he said, failing to answer my point.

"And on the other hand, I met some people recently, educated people, who said they would want to charge Christians a tax for living in Syria and to make all women cover their heads. These guys are engineers and academics – they are not from the countryside and they don't go regularly to the mosque. What's even more frightening is that before all this started happening [the unrest] they had no interest in politics, or religion and were supporters of Assad," he said.

"They plan to destroy Syria in the name of Islam? This is bullshit. These people are not Muslims – I am a Muslim. I cannot call myself the same as these people." he was in a rage now.

"This is my country and I love it more than anything, I don't want to live in Syria if Christians have to pay to live here, or if all women must be covered."

He was very fearful for his country, he said.

"You won't come to Mount Qasiun [the mountain overlooking the city] for the view. You'll come to see the bombs going off in the Christian areas and the reprisals that follow in other parts of the city.

"I want change – everybody does. But because we have many different religions, and because people are not aware of these differences in society, it will turn into civil war if we have a quick end to the current regime," he said.

"Syria is not Egypt or Tunisia," he added, referring to the largely peaceful overthrowing of dictatorships in those countries. "They have homogeneous populations."

We drove out to Dummar which was, until several years ago, a series of barren hills south west of the capital, but today is a chic up-market residential suburb. "Look at this here, what we have here is beautiful, modern. It is not like Europe but we are changing here," he sighed. "I don't want to lose this – this hope."

He told me he didn't attend the two major pro-government rallies on 30 March and the 15 June flag unfurling, but would attend another pro-regime rally the next day because he feared his country was falling apart.

"The government has almost destroyed the country but the alternative is, now, much worse because of the rising sectarian feeling I am seeing among friends and colleagues. Those taking to the streets calling for freedom do not know what they are asking for; they have no real plan for 'after'. The government has said it will introduce reforms but they need some time. The people protesting have shaken the regime but should give the government a year or two and if they haven't introduced the reforms by then they should take to the streets once more," he said.

"I will take to the streets then," he added.

We moved on to the country's social ills.

There is no difference between rich and poor in Syria, he said. I replied that of course there was.

"A wealthy man will extend the same courtesy to a poor man. The man who washes cars outside the Four Seasons hotel is referred to as 'ma'lim' or 'boss' by the guy who owns the BMW," he argued.

"The difference is between the government – and I'm including the military, the security services, those who work in ministries and other government jobs – and the rest."

Surely money plays a significant role, I suggested, it's not just about power. I said this must be wrong, because people in Syria run around for foreigners and people who appear to be wealthy.

He disagreed.

"But if the guy is driving a Mercedes with blacked out windows, he is powerful. He may not have money, the car may not even be his, but he is still a powerful man. He is a general, a chief of police, the driver for a Ministry director or the son of a well-known Alawite," he lamented.

We drove up to a park that splits the wealthy neighbourhood of Malki with Muhajareen, a conservative area which overlooks the largest Syrian flag in the city. He took a photo of the flag on his iPhone, and sighed. We began to talk about the threat of foreign intervention, as that morning an aide to the Turkish president, Abdullah Gul, said Ankara would give Syria "a week" and would then consider "foreign intervention".

"Fuck Sarkozy, screw him," he bleated when we talked about the possibility of a Libya-style intrusion in Syria.

"When the riots took place in the *banlieues* of Paris in 2005 he wouldn't take care of it for weeks [as the then French interior minister] and when he finally did, he had his police beat up and tear gas the young Arabs. Now he wants to attack Syria? He needs to mind his own business.

"But we do have a great problem in the social fabric of this country. We are all either bosses or prophets."

I asked him to explain.

"When president Shukri al-Quatli agreed to the United Arab Union with Egypt in 1958, he told Gamal Abdel Nassar [the president of Egypt at the time]: 'I'm handing over to you four million prophets and bosses.'"

He was making the point that Syrians think of themselves either as a boss or as a religious expert – and that no one knows more than they.

The wife is the boss of her kids and of her home. The husband is the boss of the house. The taxi driver, who takes the husband to work in the morning, is the boss of all taxi and all car issues. The policeman who stops the taxi driver for running a red light knows more about the law than anyone else in the land. And so on and so forth.

"Everyone thinks what they know is correct and anyone who has a differing opinion is wrong. I think 'X' and I am right. There is no space for dialogue between people in Syria and for this reason, I'm very afraid of what the future holds. This is a deeply-entrenched social position."

As for the prophets idea, when it comes to religion, be it Islam, Christianity or something else, everyone, also, is an expert, he said.

"The point," he continued, "is that people cannot sit down, listen to another's opinion and admit that that idea is better than their own. People cannot accept that they are wrong and they blame everyone else when something goes wrong. There is a sign here on the streets that says 'with freedom comes responsibility'; I don't think anyone realises with this means. We all need to take responsibility for our country and not blame the protesters or the government for our problems."

***

If the uprising had taken place ten years ago, it would in all likelihood have been dead inside a couple of weeks. There were no mobile communications companies, no internet and, vitally, no camera phones. People around the country would have had little idea of what was taking place in Deraa, in Banias and in Lattakia, outside hearsay and word of mouth, when the uprising was in its nascent stage. People would have seen what I see here in Syria every day: bus and truck loads of soldiers being transported to no one knows where, an increase in the number of military vehicles on the streets and highways around the capital, and a greater visibility of plain-clothes men brandishing automatic weapons.

The fear factor, sheer disbelief and a lack of evidence would most likely have prevailed.

Has technology made the uprising – unprecedented in forty years of Assad family rule – as successful as it has been? Probably yes, but the lack of respect for the country's youth and the lack of prospects for the future are what kept the uprising alive.

The Syrian youth are different from their parents. Forty years of economic, political and, of their own accord, social institutionalisation of the older generation saw to that. In addition, like so many other Arab countries, Syria's population has exploded, particularly since 2000, putting further pressure on the country's youth.

In Malki, a wealthy area in the west of Damascus and home to many of the city's leading business figures and politicians, members of the secret police sit in cars twenty-four hours a day. Around them are groups of local teenage boys, out smoking cigarettes, looking at cars and any passing girl. They are apolitical and do not view the sleeping men in any holistic sense. "We know who they are and why they are here but we have no problems with them, we realise they are here just to keep watch," said Samir, who lived close by and, despite his dislike of the government's policies, seemed to accept their presence, even though there was absolutely no apparent threat from unrest at the time we were there.

The role Syria's youth played in the 2011 uprising may well have been overstated by many in the English-language media.

Certainly young and internet-savvy Syrians living in other countries and concerned for their homeland contributed significantly in spreading word of the unrest by posting information and videos through Facebook, YouTube and Twitter. Of equal importance, they were able to break the language barrier by posting English translations of the crackdown in Syria onto these websites where information-starved foreign journalists awaited. However, for the most part, the young Syrians who use the internet on a daily basis were those who did not experience first-hand the regime's clampdown in the country's countryside.

And because of the socialist infrastructure the state has run on and rooted into the population over four decades, young Syrians have always had just enough to get by through help from immediate or extended family members, or even from the state. Unlike in Tunisia or Egypt, the Syrian government had done a relatively decent job of keeping the country's youth content – just about.

In the early years of Baath party control, the government established the National Union of Students, allowing the Baath to exert tight control over all student activities.

Alan George wrote in *Neither Bread nor Freedom* (2003) that the Revolutionary Youth Movement and the National Union of Students were important organisations in incorporating young people, many of whom would have been aware of the student revolts in Europe in the late 1960s, under a directly state-controlled organisation.

The 2001 decree to allow the establishment of private universities (the first, the University of Kalamoon, was founded by an organisation run by Saleem Daaboul, a wealthy businessman) has served thousands of wealthy families who do not wish to send their children – most often their daughters – overseas. Private universities, the majority of which are set on the highway between Damascus and Deraa, charge students upwards of US$10,000 per year in tuition fees.

To contrast, the state-owned and run Damascus University, which educates over 80,000 students every year, charged students 650SYP, or about US$15 dollars in 2011. In Aleppo, Syria's second city, over 60,000 students are educated each year, and in Homs and Lattakia over 100,000 students enrol, seeking a way to a better future with the funds they have available.

The establishment of the Syrian Youth Parliament by the Syrian Young Entrepreneurs Association in early March 2011, was, said several young Syrians, a move in the right direction but lacked anything substantive.

According to SANA, the government's news agency, the forum would provide "youths with a space to present their ideas regarding the various challenges facing them, particularly in the fields of education, work, environmental issues and development". No reference was made to a suggested parliamentary body, except vague mention of a committee to discuss the "internal law of the Parliament".

Samir the dentist, who applied to take part in the youth parliament, was downbeat as to whether he would be accepted. "I don't like the people who run it, but I want to try, for the sake of my country."

The 1.4 mile flag unfurled in Damascus on 15 June was supposedly initiated by a group of young people mostly from the Qassaa area of the city. What was not reported was that Qassaa is a Christian stronghold and the organisation – Syrian Youth – was formed about two weeks before the event itself and almost certainly under the patronage of the state.

SANA reported on 22 June of pro-government youth efforts in Aleppo that "included seminars and lectures by Syrian and Arab intellectuals to raise awareness among youths regarding the events and plots against Syria. The gathering youths chanted patriotic slogans and songs, raising flags and pictures of President Bashar al-Assad, in addition to repeating slogans denouncing the biased channels and their handling of the events of Syria in service of foreign agendas." This last passage gives an apt indication of the type of youth the government wanted to groom during the unrest.

The young people visible during the pro-government rallies that took place in Damascus in March and June were, for the most part, either school children, army conscripts or the families of Alawites, army officers and government officials ordered to attend to ensure a large turnout. There was little evidence on either day of spontaneous and free-willing citizens taking part.

Traffic jams caused by regime supporters in cars blocked highways and streets around the city, making it impossible for Damascenes to make it to work or to carry out weekly family house visits. Some among the apolitical masses or 'silent majority' I spoke to were, during this time and because of these events, pushed away from the regime.

However, others found themselves joining in the festivities on display by chance.

On several occasions young Christian men and women told me how they found themselves driving home or cruising around town only to join up with the rallies "just for fun". How many of these 'chance supporters' contributed to the overall number of government followers is impossible to tell but the fact that these rallies took place in the open gives the impression that this is the will of Damascus – that the entire city is behind the president. In this carnival atmosphere people thought it almost felt like everything was OK in Syria, something they needed to believe.

Others employed a different method to clear the country's troubles from their minds.

Beginning in June, the state-owned Barada Sports Club, located in Mezraah in central Damascus, opened its doors for its so-called 'Wet and Wild' pool parties. Maybe 200 young Damascenes – Christians and Muslims – partied and drank every Friday afternoon away during the summer.

Against a background of trance music, these young people could have been in St Tropez, Cancun or Las Vegas. Through cocktails and *argeleh* water pipes, bikini-clad women and tattooed men would relieve themselves from the politics dominating all conversations. Forgetting you are in troubled Syria for the US$30 entrance fee paid. Sunburn and afternoon headaches from the mix of heat and alcohol followed. These days this fragment of the Damascus youth stood shoulder to shoulder with Beirut during the July 2006 war with Israel, in terms of decadence and indifference.

These were the youths of Damascus who frequented nightclubs every Thursday night where a single drink costs US$12. The moneyed sons and daughters of businessmen, high-ranking state representatives and repatriated families, joined by a sprinkling of foreign diplomats and journalists who remained after the unrest began.

On these Friday afternoons as people in other parts of the country left the mosque to call for freedom on the streets, when hundreds were being shot for simply wanting change, politics was the farthest thing from anyone's minds. In nearby Ruk El-deen, a largely conservative neighbourhood at the foot of Mount Qasiun, in the afternoon in June when I visited gunshots could be barely heard above the din of trance music.

"We come here to forget and to have fun," one twenty-something man said. No-one else wanted to talk politics with me. It was troubling for me to think that when such things were taking place in Jisr al-Shaghour and Hama these young people were either oblivious or just did not care.

***

Edward Dark is the pseudonym of a well-known activist based in the northern city of Aleppo. Though he said he was never interested in activism or politics before the unrest of 2011, he felt he had to stand up for his country.

"Ever since we were school kids, it was repeatedly drummed into our heads never to criticise the regime or the president. In between the mandatory sticking of pictures of the president on our school books, political ideology education classes, singing his praises during the morning salute to the flag, and being force marched chanting for the regime on national holidays, the cult of personality was everywhere. The regime's grip on power is maintained by a collection of seventeen security agencies," he told me via email from Aleppo, as the road from Damascus to Aleppo was too dangerous to pass for me, a foreign journalist with visas stamped all over his passport, in June 2011 – Hama was on fire at the time. "Each agency is completely independent of the others, sometimes even a rival, from the well-known military intelligence and Air Force intelligence, to more clandestine ones simply known as branch 295 or branch 253. They are only answerable to their chief, no one else. They are above the law, and they have free rein in the country to do as they please. My own father was kidnapped by one of those agencies a few years ago; we didn't know where he was for over a week. A few months later he was let go with a simple, 'We're sorry, you were innocent,'" he wrote.

One of a few activists to remain in Syria throughout the unrest, he told me that simple criticism of a low level official was taking a risk, as one never knew how connected he may have been, and, in Syria, the name of the game is connections. "It doesn't matter what rank you are in any institution, or even your seniority, it's all about the people you know. The higher up you knew, the more you could do. They [the authorities] could arrest judges, MPs, policemen, ministers anyone they pleased, without a warrant and without notifying anyone. If they died from torture under detention, so be it, their bodies were sent home and their families were warned to shut up."

Dark, who was also the editor of the website Syrialeaks.com, went on to say *wasta* (contacts) could be used for anything from cancelling a parking ticket, to landing you a multi-million dollar contract, to a "get out of jail free card".

"I was never involved in any activism before the Syrian uprising began, I knew people who were, though, and I always thought they were very brave. Many who were active before the uprising began used their real names and they have all been to jail at least once – no exceptions. Some are still in jail serving sentences for trumped up charges such as 'weakening the national spirit' and 'attacking the prestige of the state', others are jailed for spying or collaborating with foreign states, such as Tal el-Malouhi," said Dark, referring to the eighteen-year-old girl jailed for supposedly posting critical comments of the regime on a blog and was sentenced to five years by a Syrian court for 'spying'.

During the unrest, he told me, smart people shut up and went about their own business, smarter people made alliances with corrupt officials and siphoned off public money in full view. The rest suffered in silence.

Dark used Twitter and YouTube to get word of the uprising out. As an activist, he relied on a series of informal contact links to source information about the military and security crackdowns that took place around the country.

"When organising demonstrations on the ground, it was first coordinated with calls to protest on the main revolution page on Facebook [in February 2011]. After the uprising took off, it was a given protests would always take place outside mosques after Friday prayers."

He told me there was a level of vetting involved when he received information or videos via social media – a decision must be reached about whether the information can be trusted or not.

"The more 'votes' it gets and the more other information appears to back it up, the more we spread it. If it's proved fake or unreliable, it will die down or be discredited by us, as the regime sometimes purposely tries to plant false news and videos. Obviously the better known and trusted activists get a bigger say," he said.

"For example, I might receive an eye-witness account or a video from a friend of mine in Hama; I would then email it to my inner circle of trusted friends and then post it up on Twitter. This gets information from Hama out to the wider activist body, in the same way, I don't have any reliable people I know personally in Homs, but a friend of mine does and I would receive information about that city from him." According to Dark, activists in Syria are organised into loose circles or groups, usually by virtue of geographic location.

Dark also used Facebook and Skype. "For example, we use a combination of TOR, proxies, tunnels and VPNs [virtual private networks] to surf the web, and we talk in code when using mobile phones. Due to the nature of the way we operate, information passes from one group to another through people from one group whom the other group trusts. These connections may be mutual friends, or long-time activists. This sometimes means that information may be sketchy or even inaccurate, but this is the only way we have and it has worked out well so far."

Dark knew many people who had been detained and arrested during the protests. Some, he said, for filming protests, some for posting them online, and some for saying something they shouldn't have on their mobile phones. "Two of my cousins were arrested for protesting, both were released after a few days and after being made to sign pledges not to protest again," he said.

Others had been forced to work for the government by posting to pro-regime pages and websites upon release. "Owners of internet cafés are made to spy on clients using government supplied software, and there have been quite a few arrests at internet cafés. Usually, detained people get released in no more than two weeks, after being subjected to threats, intimidation, psychological pressure, and beatings. In some cases, serious torture and abuse occurs."

He said he led a normal daily life and went to work as usual. In a cat and mouse game, camouflage is the best weapon. "A lot of us are like this, I'll even appear to be a staunch pro-regime supporter on occasions, it is all part of playing along with the charade and the facade the regime likes to keep up, where people praise it on the outside, but secretly curse it under their breaths."

Dark believed that the 2011 uprising was the beginning of the end of this regime, at least in its current form. He thought it simply could not continue functioning as it was, that there could be no return to the 'business as usual' of before.

"It's just a question of time, if this round of protests gets subdued then another round will flare up again pretty soon, the seeds of dissent have already been sown in Syria."

**

Tourism accounted for US$8.4 billion, through over 8.5 million foreign visits to Syria in 2010. With this sector – a lifeblood for the country's youth – and now destroyed, their prospects are fewer still.

Those hoping to score summer internships among the country's once-blooming banking sector saw their prospects evaporate. Every sector of the economy, from cafés to aluminium factories, laid off staff.

Even if there had been no uprising in Syria, the state's inability to support the huge number of students graduating every summer meant it would have had to introduce a new programme to help people find jobs, and soon. For years analysts have been claiming that "sooner or later" the government will have to address this issue, and they are correct, with over 200,000 gradu-ates spilling into the job pool each year. The economic system in Syria in 2011 would have been swamped by the middle of the decade. The problems afflicting the youth of Syria were coming for the regime, sooner or later.

There were other disquieting events involving young people – kids on one occasion – and the denial that existed in one rural community not far from Damascus. One Saturday in late June a family friend showed me a video clip from his mobile phone. The video showed him, a fourteen-year-old Christian, along with about a dozen other children from his street in a village thirty-five kilometres from the capital. Some of the children partak-ing in this mini-rally were smaller than the flags and portraits of Bashar al-Assad they were carrying. Nearby, mothers called on them to go around the corner and come back. The children smiled, almost embarrassed to be filmed on camera.

The children had no real idea of what they were doing. They were too young to know exactly what they were calling for.

It was one of the most unsettling scenes I have seen. I couldn't help but think of children in Nazi Germany who, in utter inno-cence, participated in similar rallies declaring their love for Ad-olf Hitler.

***

Laila met me at a café in downtown Damascus. She was from a wealthy family that lived in Dummar, a suburb on the north-western outskirts of Damascus. She was twenty-one years old and in her third year of media studies at Damascus University.

"I saw some students from my class take off their belts and hit medicine students who wanted to hold a demonstration for freedom. It was shocking. Almost everyone in my class is totally pro-government. I've cut thirty of my friends from Facebook be-cause I can't continue to listen to their rubbish. I'm not talking to two of my cousins because they disagree with me." The thing that had surprised her most, she said, was how educated peo-ple she knew were talking about the crisis. "They're saying we should all stand blindly behind the government."

I suggested that they were probably afraid of civil war in Syria. Laila disagreed.

"In Jordan there are Palestinians that follow various Palestinian groups, there are Jordanians, Bedouins, Christians and so on and they get along. The sectarian idea doesn't have to apply to Syria."

She told me how on 15 June, on the day of the unfurling of a giant Syrian flag in the Mezzah area of Damascus, she had an exam at the nearby faculty of literature. "I had to take off my shoes to cross the street because I couldn't walk on the flag in order to get to my exam. Then when I started the test I couldn't concentrate because of the noise from the rally outside. I mean, what type of logic and thinking is this – to hold a huge government rally next to a state university where state exams are taking place? It is just so stupid.

"My house was worth seventy million Syrian pounds [almost US$1.5 million at the time] before the unrest began – we have money, we have a lot to lose. But we will gain more under a different government. My four brothers have to go to live and work in Dubai because they can't get work here and because of the military service. The government is driving its youth away."

Sipping on a lemon-mint drink, Laila was convinced Syria was being held back by those in power.

"We have to work all year to spend one week in Beirut for some fun. What is this? Beirut is nothing, we could have so much more right here in Syria," she said, bending marks into her drinking straw in frustration.

Laila said she has been once or twice to Beirut for shopping and to visit pubs and that her closest four or five friends all shared her opinion on 'The Situation'.

She also told me of the mafia-style workings of the police and security apparatus as the regime worked to stamp out dissent across the country in July.

"My friend's father was detained in Hama one month ago [May 2011]. Very few people know this, but US$2,000 will allow you to find out where a person is being held. US$4,000 will ensure he or she stays alive although it does not guarantee his or her health. US$2,000 more will get him or her on a list for question-ing which will mean, at some stage, he or she will be released."

She said she would like to see foreign military intervention in Syria to kick out the regime.

"The regime will never give in because of the system they have organised. I don't think they will change as they are say-ing. I would prefer to die by an American or English gun than by someone from my own country."

For Laila, as for others, corruption and the necessity of *wasta* are hated aspects of daily life in Syria. Corruption and bureau-cracy angered her most.

"If I want to get a passport in Jordan it would take me one hour. In Syria it will take forever unless I pay the employee some money.

"My father goes twice a week to an electricity office. When he goes there he has three assistants and they're all from the 86 area [a predominantly Alawite-inhabited area in west Damas-cus]. This is the state's disease, this is how they have worked for decades. It is unsustainable and it needs to be rooted out and ended."

She said the magazine office where she worked part-time was empty. "There are no employees. Companies have stopped spending money on advertising so the magazine simply has no revenue. It's as simple as that."

She went on to talk about the business situation in Syria and the anger it made her feel.

"Do you know how they started Syriatel?" she asked me, refer-ring to the telecommunications company owned by the presi-dent's cousin. "Anyone who wanted to open a mobile phone line had to pay 10,000 Syrian pounds and then wait for months. Then they bought the equipment and technology they needed and started their own company. What rubbish! This is the peo-ple's company. Those people did not pay for it yet they call it their own.

"Do you know why there are no Starbucks, no McDonald's and so on in Syria? If I want to start a business I need to give the government 51 per cent ownership. They then take another 10 per cent of the profits from me. So essentially they have 61 per cent of my company. Why would anyone want to open a business in this situation? This is why we are such an undeveloped country."

She told me about the reasons for social inequality in Syria.

"The people who live in 86, the Alawites who have free phone lines and who don't ever pay for their electricity, are being told they are going to be attacked and are being given guns by the security forces 'to protect themselves'.

"We have laws but no one obeys them. Why? Because they are not being enforced. People are flexible. If the government leads with a bad example the people will follow.

"People in Dubai or Beirut don't throw litter on the street, but here we do. Why? I know that if I talk on the phone while driving and a policeman stops me I can give him a smile, slip 500 Syrian pounds [US$10] into my driving licence and smile. He'll let me go."

I asked her whether it wasn't the responsibility of the people not to do this, not to give out money to the police and other government workers and not to throw litter in the streets.

"My mother was in the US two months ago and she told me how in one mall there was a green space where people could not sit. In Syria, everyone would sit there for two reasons. One, because they don't take the average policeman or, for example, Ministry inspector seriously. Second, because they simply have nowhere else to go. We have lots of fancy restaurants for rich people but nothing has been put in place for the poor who want to have fun."

Laila said she was neither an activist nor part of the opposition beyond posting cryptic remarks on her Facebook page. I asked her for the solution to the current unrest.

"We need to turn the clock back to zero. Sure it will take time, maybe five years, but it will certainly be worth it. We have been led as sheep for forty years and if this government stays we will be sheep for forty more."

I told her that I thought this was the danger. "If you have a sheep that has been following a shepherd for three years and you let him go free he'll be dead in a week."

She was visibly angry as she waved my point away:

"I believe that everyone has one chance. The regime has had chances for forty years. They've had so many chances since the problems started in March but what have they done? Nothing. They must go."

Laila's story was being repeated in conversations among thousands of young people across the country. Some wanted the status quo to be maintained so that they would have a job, any job. Others wanted a system overhaul and see the regime as the principal obstacle to achieving that.

It was not until I experienced the fearless voice of young people seeking a new future for their country in the heart of Damascus that I fully realised what was at stake for the youth.

***

On 30 June, I took a microbus from my house to meet a friend in the Baramkeh area of the city. The bus dropped me close to the faculty of economics in Damascus University where I would walk for five minutes under a blazing sun and through shops selling stationery to meet him at his place of work. It was a Thursday and at 3pm students were exiting the gates of the campus after finishing their summer exams. Some chatted in small groups, others leaned over car doors making plans for the weekend. They walked out past the bored-looking armed guards like they didn't exist. Sometimes the guards asked to see student identification, sometimes they did not.

Just that morning I had been thinking that once the authorities stopped shooting and shelling the protesters – which they largely had at that time – the momentum the demonstrators had gained, mostly because of the government's nationwide crackdown against them, would be lost. Only minutes later, I was to be proved wrong in the most startling of ways. That afternoon was to be the first time I saw the brutal tactics of the regime first-hand. It was one of the first instances of verifiable government heavy-handedness against peaceful protesters anywhere in Syria. But perhaps most importantly of all, it stood as a reminder of the will of the youth.

Before I reached the gates of the faculty of economics – about one hundred metres from where the microbus dropped me – I heard a sound so unbelievable it shook me.

Just as I looked up, a small group of people had joined together next to a kiosk and started shouting '*hurria, hurria*'. I thought I was dreaming. They were calling 'freedom, freedom'. Bystanders looked on at the crowd in utter amazement, unsure whether they should run away or maybe join in.

Pro-government rallies were common at this time in Damascus but to see people shouting for the opposition in the heart of the city in the heart of Damascus was unfathomable. The university was under twenty-four-hour armed guard. Army-registered cars were parked at the gates day and night. One female protester among about one hundred others managed to unfurl a poster which I could not read in time before police and security forces charged on the crowd. The student protesters fled like flies. Some were beaten by the baton-wielding *mukhabarat* but managed to escape. Others were caught and detained by the plain-clothed men. The whole thing lasted no more than thirty seconds. But the students, with this incredible act of bravery, had got their message out to all within earshot.

As I looked on – no more than twenty metres from where the group had formed – I turned into the nearest shop so as not to be identified as the students ran away from the police. Some followed me into the shop and at this point I was fearful of being identified as one of the protesters. A foreign journalist at the scene of a student protest. What would the authorities have thought? Would they have believed that it was down to pure chance that I happened to be there, passing through on the way to meet a friend? Surely not. It was too much of a coincidence.

"You want freedom? I'll show you freedom after a while," I heard a security officer telling a student as he led him away in handcuffs no more than two feet from me.

Other demonstrators were pinned against footpaths and were beaten with batons.

As the students fled in panic into nearby shops and down residential alleyways, I caught up with a protester, who ran down a street that was also home to a building housing Baath party offices. His face was cut to pieces. The outside of his right arm bled incessantly. He told me he couldn't find several of his friends and feared for their safety. I told him and another student who joined him to be careful. As we turned a corner together – by chance – I saw an employee of the Central Bank of Syria looking directly at us. He was waiting to enter his English language class and I knew him because my friend was his teacher. The bank employee was on the phone. I wanted to speak further to the students, to ask how and why they organised the protest, to find out if they planned any more. But the bank employee knew who I was. I had to leave the students for my own safety. The boy was clearly bloodied and for me to be seen with him, talking at length, would have put me in great danger.

The university campus was closed off immediately after the protest as police searched out hiding protesters. Later that Thursday evening, police and army cars patrolled the university area.

Demonstrations not on a Friday and away from the relative security of mosques were extremely rare in the Syrian capital at that time and the protest, though small, portrayed a youth unwilling to accept the will of a regime coming under increasing pressure from anti-government feeling in the capital.

It was a brutal attempt at suppressing a clearly peaceful demonstration, and the authorities' reaction to the protest bore a stark contrast to the line being taken by the regime, which repeatedly stated that Syrians had a right to participate in peaceful protests.

For me, who had for months viewed demonstrations and police brutality on Arab satellite television, and could never entirely accept these videos as being fully accurate, seeing with my own eyes the brutal and uncompromising reaction of the authorities to this clearly peaceful protest abolished any doubt I had held.

For the majority of young people in Syria, freedom or living in a democratic state is not an end goal in itself, despite the images of protesters in Syria calling for the downfall of the regime appearing on television screens around the world.

Syria's youth want respect. They do not want to be afraid of saying the wrong thing in front of the wrong person that may see their job, or themselves, taken away.

They want a chance to contribute to their country without having to pay the first six months of their salary as a bribe just to get work in the first place. They want to feel like they have learned something after four years in university.

Perhaps most of all, Syria's youth want an end to the corruption, the nepotism, the culture of *wasta* – all the things that make starting a new life in Syria so taxing.

Many English-language publications claim that President Assad is a favourite among the country's young. He is. The vast majority don't want anyone else, because, to some extent, there is no one else they feel can lead the country they care for so deeply.

Speaking to these young people has made one thing clear to me: they will not lie down, like their parents did for decades. They feel change on the horizon and want a piece of it. They know that not all people want the same thing, but realise the system in Syria is broken.

VII

BEING A FOREIGNER, A RESIDENT AND A JOURNALIST IN THE REVOLT

Working as a journalist in Syria through the revolt was an exercise in patience, judgement and nerve-control. Maintaining impartiality when editors called seeking only comments and interviews with protestors, and coverage of what the regime was doing to quash the revolt, contrasted sharply with the largely peaceful Damascus streets and busy cafés. I heard contrasting viewpoints on the nature and motivation behind the uprising, depending on who I spoke to: many Sunnis cursed the regime, most Christians cursed the protestors and secularists cursed them both. Some made significant points; as civil conflict became increasingly likely towards the end of 2011 few continued to listen to opposing opinions. Attempting to form a balanced opinion in this environment was difficult and I decided I could believe only what I saw. At times it was also a deeply traumatic and dangerous experience. For me, dealing with the regime's security apparatus had always been tricky – and where was the red line? During the revolt, the red line ebbed and flowed each day. A new media law meant, in theory, greater freedom to do my job; the government signing the Arab League peace deal in November, likewise. But many local and foreign journalists were detained and deported. Operating in this most fluid of environments was intensely testing. I would print my by-line when I supposed the topic of the article was not something to attract the negative attention of the security forces or the Ministry for Information, which granted visas for foreign journalists. Consequently, I put my name to articles reporting the unveiling of a huge Syrian flag in Damascus in June 2011, or the 23 December bombings in the capital, or an article documenting the thoughts and actions of the business community.

On the street, my grasp of Damascene Arabic was enough to allow me to pass as a local. I acted as others did when taking public transport: one of the best ways to avoid unwanted stares when taking taxis was to exclaim "*Ya rub!*" ("Oh, God!") when sitting in the passenger seat. I would immediately be perceived as a Syrian. If the taxi driver talked and I said nothing in reply he would presume I didn't want to engage in conversation. On microbuses I stared at what other passengers stared at, I tutted when others did. I often played the fool, emphasising that I worked for a business newspaper in benign Ireland when dealing with the security services, border officials or government organs.

Back at the beginning, as Egypt burned and word of protest spread from Libya, Bahrain and Yemen, a Facebook page titled 'Syrian Revolution 2011' called for a 'Day of Rage' on 4 and 5 February.

It was an astounding piece of news. No one knew who was organising the 'protest'. Fewer in Syria knew if it would actually happen. No one spoke about it openly. (As it turned out, the page was run by Fida el-din el-Sayyed of the Muslim Brotherhood, who lived in Sweden at the time.) Protests were to take place outside the parliament in central Damascus and at Merjah square downtown. Of course, the security services knew more about these plans than most.

The night before, a Thursday and the beginning of the weekend in Syria, a group of cars – BMWs, old Mercedes and SUVs – drove through the streets of Damascus beeping horns and waving flags and photos of the president. The car registration plates made it obvious that they were state-owned – the words *jeysh* (army) and *shurta* (police) written in green on the plates indicated the vehicles belonged to the army or the police. On the streets a light rain began to fall as startled shoppers and teens looked on.

The next day – the first Day of Rage – I sat at a café on Abed street, close to the parliament, for a couple of hours filing several hundred words as the rain spilled down outside. I pitched and was commissioned to write for the *Irish Times* and the *Sunday Business Post*. The streets were silent but anyone with ears knew about the Facebook call to freedom. In the early afternoon I took a walk through the Hamra shopping district close to the parliament to buy cigarettes. There was almost no one around, unsurprising given the rain, though there were security men standing on several street corners.

At around 4pm I took a green bus (the ones later used to transport *shabiha* and security forces around the country on Fridays) to Bab Touma. The route across town took me past Merjah square and saw me pass one side of the parliament, a French-era building sitting on the corner of a main thoroughfare and a shopping street. The bus was half full and as we passed Merjah dozens of men in the ubiquitous black jackets were standing around; but there were no protestors. A friend who was in Merjah square two hours before said he saw snipers on the roofs of the buildings surrounding the square: the regime had prepared even when the protestors had not. In Christian Bab Touma the only thing out of the ordinary was the rain. I immediately boarded another bus back to my base at the café. Passing through the city centre's main streets, all was quiet. As we passed the parliament the passengers in the bus all looked left to see if anything out of the ordinary was taking place. There was nothing, save a dozen or so men smoking and getting wet in the rain. That night dozens of regime cars once more filled the streets waving flags and beeping horns. The call for protest, it seemed, had fallen on deaf ears.

***

A little over a month later the first protestors were gunned down in Deraa on 18 March. A small demonstration in Souk Hamadiyeh in central Damascus saw dozens detained. Dissent grew. In the months that followed the protests and consequent crackdown grew in all corners of the country. In May, Noor called me up. "I have some people you might want to talk to."

On the rooftop café at Sham City Centre in Kafr Souseh, Noor and her western-dressed friend met me. It was May and the summer heat had yet to arrive. It being my first time at the café, I was particularly nervous. I didn't know its regular clientele, its layout, whether it had the capacity for facilitating conversations such as the one we were about to open. However, it was almost empty save for a group of middle-aged women chatting and drinking Turkish coffee on an outdoor patio. Noor's girlfriend left and two young men arrived.

This was only the second time I had met Noor and I had little idea if she was to be trusted. She told me to turn off my phone. Earlier the same morning, Mohammed, Noor's friend, said he walked twenty kilometres through forests north of Deraa to evade the authorities after his parents were arrested by security forces. He feared that if he did not leave Deraa, he would be next. He had been caught taking video footage of soldiers who had been patrolling the city. "The soldiers took my identification card," he said. Several days later security men showed up at his home. "They said that if I keep quiet and they hear nothing about me for the next four days, then they will release my mother from prison," said Mohammed, who, like many, would only speak to me on condition of anonymity. "If my name comes up, they said they will kill her." Mohammed said he did not know where his parents were being held.

By May, thousands of people from Deraa and the surrounding area had been detained. "They are holding them in schools and in the main stadium in the city," Mohammed said. "No one has been allowed to go to mosques to pray for weeks." He added that his family was well-regarded and had influence in the area. "But in this situation, it no longer counts," he said.

By now there was a group of three young men with Noor. They looked intently at me as I listened on. They were both fearful and intrigued.

Marwan, a university student from Deraa, had also recently fled the town for Damascus. "The security came to my family's house looking for me last week. My father told them I was in

Beirut studying. They came after me because my sister's friend was arrested and he gave my name as being his friend," he said. Marwan said he was hiding out among friends in the Syrian capital, moving from house to house. Amer, a twenty-two-year-old law student also from Deraa, said he didn't know whether to be hopeful or despairing about the path his country had taken. "We wish we had the situation in Libya," he said, referring to free Benghazi. "At least they have some feeling of freedom, we are afraid. But I think there is no way back now."

I turned my phone back on and Mohammad sent me three videos he had taken inside Deraa via his mobile phone. A little later on I watched them. The videos depicted scenes of devastation inside Deraa. Filmed from the back seat of a car, one video shows trucks on fire and others blackened by smoke. Car windows are smashed. Footpaths, telephone poles and cars are crushed by what must have been a tank. As the car turned a corner, bullets struck the wall of a house. Another house close by had its entire second floor walls destroyed, probably by a rocket. Further on, on the corner of a street, another car smashed by a tank, walls and a shop gutted by fire come into view. The people in the car cursed the regime. "Look at our Deraa!" said one man. As the car approaches a checkpoint manned by a tank the video ends.

***

At all times I was prepared, mentally, for someone to call to the door and to say: "We are taking you to the airport and you will never come back to Syria because you are telling lies about our country."

But the security services were usually more thoughtful that this – they would call me ahead. "Hello, is this Stephen Starr?"

"Yes, who is this?"

"You live in Jdaydieh Artouz, right?"

"Yes," I replied, trying to speak further before being cut off.

"Where exactly?" he asked.

"Close to the Kemal hospital; but who is this?"

"OK; I will see you at Kemal hospital in fifteen minutes. Is your house close by?"

There was no point resisting. I was quite sure who he was.

"Yes, it is, but who am I speaking to?"

"My name is Abu Ali. OK, see you in fifteen minutes."

And the line went dead.

In the fifteen minutes before I scrambled to meet Abu Ali I gave the number of the Irish consulate and the USB with all my writings to a friend. At the time there was little else I could do. I walked down the stairs and out onto the main street, my heart thumping in my ears. I expected to see a group of men sitting in a blacked-out car but there were none. A man sitting in a Suzuki pick-up van looked directly across the street at me, but I took little notice of this – in Syria everyone stares. Then my phone rang. The call was coming from the man in the pick-up.

A stout, grim and serious figure, Abu Ali asked if my house was far. I pointed to the entrance gate. "It's just over there," I said, attempting to look calm. I was shaking now, trying to control my body. I had been writing about the revolution for months and perhaps he knew this. He parked up the Suzuki and followed me upstairs and into my house.

He took out a notebook and asked me a series of ancillary questions. "What's your father's name? What's your mother's name? What do they do? What newspaper do you work for? Where is the office in Syria?" There is no office, I told him, slightly baffled at his questions. I knew he was with the intelligence services but I had no idea why he was at my house. Did he want to arrest or detain me? Was he there just to let me know that they knew where I was? Had they seen my emails? Maybe he wanted to plant a bugging device.

He left after ten minutes, refusing tea or coffee, and giving no explanation about who he was, why he had come or what he intended to do with the information – most likely useless – I had given him.

Without doubt his intention was to instil in me a semblance of fear. The point was to tell me, "Look, we know exactly where you are and we're monitoring you, so don't mess around."

Several weeks later I went to the local *mukhtar*, the man whose job it is to register all residents in a particular town or neighbourhood. All foreigners are required to register here, too.

The *mukhtar* documents a variety of details including phone numbers, addresses, parents' names and occupation, scrawled in pen on a single page. On this occasion I went there, a ten-minute walk from my house, to get a paper proving I lived in the area, which I needed for my residency application.

Abu Said, a deep-voiced, polite man, smiled at me. He remembered me from before.

I went in, sat down and lit a cigarette. There was a man sitting opposite me going through a notebook that contained a list of names. Abu Said was also going through his own book. When the man closed the book and left on a motorcycle, I realised what they were doing: the individual sitting opposite was from the *mukhabarat* and was searching for the addresses of people the security was looking for, probably because they were involved in protests. "This is how they do it!" I screamed inside. "This is how they catch the protestors!"

With all these thoughts going around my head I began to fidget and appear nervous. My uneasiness was picked up on by Abu Said, but he said nothing. I gulped down the bitter coffee, thanked him and left.

I was registered with the Ministry for Information, the passports office and my friends Abu Ali and Samer (another agent who came to my house to interview me in January 2011) in the *mukhabarat*; did this mean that because they knew I was a legitimate journalist, I could afford to be more obvious in my daily activities? Or did it mean the opposite? Because I was upfront and on their records, did it mean I was the one of the first names they looked for when bad press was being reported about Syria? The fact that the Ministry for Information called up my editor at *Forward* magazine in late September to ask if I wrote for them didn't make me any more, or less, sure but it did heighten my anxiety. *Forward's* editor asked the official if I was in trouble. The official answered that I was not, that the Ministry was "just checking up" on me. It was a constant battle of wits and a fight against paranoia.

By late summer 2011, the army began building high reinforced concrete walls around its army bases on the south west outskirts of Damascus. In other parts of Syria the security forces and the army handed out guns and sandbags to Alawites. For me and the rest of the country, watching soldiers pour concrete into reinforcement barriers on the side of highways, the message we were getting was that the regime was fearing and preparing for the worst – attacks on its military instalments, the outbreak of civil war, even. For the Alawites, Christians and other minorities, seeing these new high walls vindicated their perspective that both the country and the regime were under attack from 'armed terrorist gangs' – why else would they be taking such measures, thought many. However, these efforts were largely to instil a sense of fear among Syria's chief minority populations – those the regime depended upon most to keep them in power, to turn up at pro-regime rallies.

Country roads were perpetually heavy with military traffic, a marked change from pre-uprising times. At the Soumarieh bus station, trucks transporting cattle carcasses and huge sacks of rice made their way to the military camps outside the town of Qatana. Civilians looked on with anger: inflation saw food prices increase by over 50 per cent. The same day, a couple of kilometres out of the capital, I and the other passengers on my microbus were treated to the sight of a team of soldiers pushing a broken-down, dilapidated army truck that had cut out on the side of the road. Two hundred metres further up the road, an old, olive green army bus lay standing at an unnatural angle – its tyres were punctured and it was simply abandoned. By late summer it was easy to distinguish between the old army vehicles and the BMWs, Hondas and Volkswagens that belonged to the security.

Some people pitied the soldiers, others loathed them. More differentiated between the young, uneducated, poor boys, like those pushing the broken down truck, and those driving the BMWs – who were members of the security and intelligence organisations and almost certainly always Alawite.

In May, when the town of Madamiyeh was cut off from the rest of the world by checkpoints and tanks, a friend called.

"Don't try to go home from Damascus this evening – there are checkpoints at Madamiyeh and they're asking everyone for their IDs." At the time I had not yet been issued an official journalist visa – I had nothing on my person to say I needed to pass through the checkpoint in order to go home. Being a foreigner in Damascus was seen as relatively normal, but perhaps a little surprising. However, venturing outside the city was something few foreigners or Damascenes would do at this time. What excuse did I have?

I decided against trying to explain to soldiers where I was going and why I had no ID with me, in favour of staying in the city centre with a South African friend, Justin (not his real name).

At Justin's house I flick through his back copies of *National Geographic*. Rainforests, polar bears, ultra-modern buildings. Tremendous images. Given the rapid changes occurring around me in the real world, the pre-revolt Syria was as much a reality as that polar bear looking back at me from the magazine. It felt like a surreal dream. I couldn't get home, there were checkpoints and soldiers on the highways. I was separated from my passport and didn't know whether I would have to send someone to retrieve it for me. I had no idea when I could return to my house.

Justin had jazz music playing in the background. I complimented him on his apartment, a duplex house with a roof that opened onto the Damascus night sky. He told me he wanted to buy the apartment, largely because he had his sights set on marriage to a daughter of Damascus and in this land having a house well in advance of marriage was a prerequisite. He told me of the difficulties he was facing in trying to get his sweetheart's family to allow him to marry her. "They [the family] don't want me to take her away to another country. Her father won't even hear my name mentioned."

We went out to get some sandwiches. I wanted a burger but the bakery that makes the round bread was closed. "Why?" I asked the waiter. "Because it is in Madamiyeh," said the man behind the counter. "What happened out there?" I asked, looking to see if he knew something I didn't. "It's closed off, they're not making or sending any bread," he replied.

I slept on Justin's floor wondering when, or even if, I would be able to get back to my house.

The next evening I called my friend Omar, who lived in Hajar Aswad, close to the Palestinian camp of Yarmouk, to see if I could stay with him that night as the checkpoints along the highway at Madamiyeh were still up.

"Of course; just bring yourself; we have whiskey to finish," he said.

I took a microbus down through the south of the capital from the open Deraa highway into the narrow, winding, traffic-clogged streets that characterise this part of the city. The bus took me along the outside of the Yarmouk camp, where elderly men sat out on plastic chairs smoking *argeleh*, facing an open, grassless field, before turning left, back into the crowds of residential life. Second-hand car shops lined both sides of the street. Footpaths were non-existent and traffic lights barely visible through years of accumulated dust. The micro plunged on through the traffic and I got off at Hajar Aswad, close to the Palestine Hospital.

I bought a large plate of chicken stew from a nearby fast food restaurant. Omar, who only a couple of months earlier spent two nights in prison after being arrested – wrongly he said – for drinking in public, had whiskey and *arak*.

"Stephen, the regime has too many cards to play to feel really threatened by these protestors," Omar, a translator, told me before I was able to sit down. "They know they can control the international community. For example, if the West pressures the government with military intervention the government can stand up and say 'OK, if you stay out of our affairs we will give up supporting Hamas and Hezbollah'. They may even say that they will sign a peace deal with Israel," he said, inhaling the smoke from his Winston cigarette.

"The interesting point is this: the regime does not have to follow through on these promises, all it has to do is to say it will and the other countries will back off and allow the regime to keep killing people."

One of Omar's friends had found on YouTube a revolutionary song dedicated to those who had died at the hands of the state. All fell silent before one shouts out: "Turn this off; it is too sad, let's not remember what's going on." Omar jumped up to play a video of Louis Armstrong's 'Hit the Road, Jack'. Louis was still smiling wide when 'What a Wonderful World' was played. All in the small bedroom fell silent again. Shortly after, with the whiskey almost finished, Omar's friends file out the door. There was no hope in their words, their faces. None were convinced of their own predictions of where the country will go.

The next day the checkpoint at Madamiyeh was taken down. I boarded a micro at the SANA building in central Damascus and went home. Along the way we saw soldiers and tanks, tents and military vehicles parked along the highway north of the town. All shop fronts, usually teeming with children kicking footballs and men stooping over used cars, were closed behind shutters. The evening prayer call had just sounded out and old men dressed in the white *dishdashas* were uneasily making their way to a white-stoned mosque perched on the side of the highway. Those of us in the micro stared into the alleys and at the tanks and soldiers. No one said a word.

About a week later the entire length of highway that bordered Madamiyeh was closed. No one knew what went on inside. Commuters going to and from Damascus had to take a southern route through back roads. On this road tanks were parked up facing north into Madamiyeh. Soldiers patrolled the road where omnipresent police and army barracks were located. Mobile phone coverage was down. But no one stopped to see what was happening to the people inside. No one cared enough. All were too fearful.

***

During the three-day Eid holiday that followed Ramadan in August, I returned to Qatana, south west of the capital, to visit a friend. Leaving his home in the early evening, I walked down the street to wait for a micro. Tensions were high in Qatana at that time. At the top of the town on a street that passes from east to west, I spotted a pick-up, an ambulance and an old military jeep driving at speed about 300 metres from me. I thought little of it and was more concerned with the quiet in the streets.

A couple of blacked out security cars moved slowly, like the local cats, into and out of the Christian neighbourhoods. After a long wait a micro appeared and I got on. We travelled the usual route down through the town and over east to an area called Ashara. Everywhere dissent was visible through the black patches of paint covering anti-Assad graffiti. One kilometre on was the main roundabout entrance to the town where a checkpoint was manned by three tanks, a dozen or so soldiers and as many plain-clothes security men carrying AK47s. Just before the roundabout I spotted the ambulance, then the jeep and then the pick-up again. I was certain they are the same ones that I saw fifteen minutes previously. Then all necks in the micro craned to the right: a large bearded man in civilian clothes was shoving two boys – aged in their late teens and about half his size – into the ambulance. The micro did not slow down or stop. No one spoke. Instead we drove on to the roundabout where hands went into pockets for IDs as we drew up to a checkpoint.

"I'm Irish," I told the security officer, who was not dressed in military fatigues, when he got to me. He was looking through my passport and I prayed he didn't see one of the many journalist visas. Just one had the word *sahafi* or 'journalist' in Arabic and I knew they generally cannot read English.

"What are you doing here? Are you here on holiday?" he asked, keen to get moving through the other passengers and to allow us to drive on. Judging by the way the two young boys were being handled, they had more immediate concerns.

"I live in the next town, I'm visiting friends here," I said.

He wasn't even looking at me anymore and was instead pulling ID cards from the passengers behind me. The speed at which he moved bordered on carelessness, but clearly all passengers were fearful of him. His blue eyes scanned rapidly through names and addresses before he swiped his arm out of the window. We pulled away past the poorly-constructed checkpoint and off into the Syrian night. My sigh of relief must have been audible to those sitting around me. Without doubt the most uncomfortable part of this episode was watching the *mukhabarat* agent checking the passengers in front of me and waiting for my turn. Presenting him with an Irish passport, I was sure to ring alarm bells.

I had waited for his face to betray his confusion. The passengers around me had been as bewildered as the security officer.

By then, in late August, getting stopped at checkpoints while travelling in microbuses had become something resembling normality. Earlier in the summer I was stopped in a microbus outside Soumarieh, the southern bus station that served travellers to Jordan and Lebanon, as well as dozens of villages and towns in southern and western Syria. On that occasion, only the men had been ordered to present their IDs. A passenger sitting in front of me passed his ID to the security officer at the door, who called out each passenger's name to another man sitting under a tree at the side of the road. He checked what must have been a list of wanted names, of men on the run or accused of conspiring against the regime. The man under the tree signalled no and we drove onwards into Damascus.

In the autumn and winter months, I drove past the security personnel posted at checkpoints around Qatana on a weekly basis. The same faces greeted me on the way into the town, and at the checkpoint going out. "Where are you from – Germany?" asked a middle-aged soldier with a mouth half emptied of teeth. He clearly was unable to read the details on my passport. "No, I'm from Ireland," I replied when he stopped me in October. "Which country is better – Ireland or Syria?" he asked. "*Walla*, Syria is much better, the sun is always shining, it is not as expensive here," I said. He let me through and I felt genuinely relieved to have had this short chat with him. After I had showed my passport a couple of times the checkpoint guards knew both my face and the car, and let me pass without any trouble. It was clear that these men were human. They spent shifts of at least twelve hours standing on the roads checking for weapons. But they were well trained. On one occasion in early December 2011, the same security officer who checked traffic leaving the town even stopped an army jeep and looked around inside. At the time, the Free Syria Army was growing in numbers and boldness in the area, probably because of locally defecting soldiers. For New Year's Eve the security agents upped the ante. They were new, which meant they didn't know me, so there were complications. "You're originally Syrian?" he asked in Arabic. "No, I'm

Irish." This time I was driving. He leafed through my passport but clearly didn't understand a word. He asked me where I was going and the name of the family. I told him but, unlike the previous security agents, his face stayed blank. He asked what I did and I told him I was an English teacher. He asked me to get out of the car and check the boot. I had seen the drivers ahead of me do similarly and as a result, I was relatively calm. I knew by now that if I stayed calm and acted as if the entire procession was a regular part of life I was likely to get away with escape using this false identity. He looked to see if there was anything inside but the boot was empty. The encounter ended with an apology in English from the guard and I drove off towards Qatana.

Later the same evening, at exactly midnight, there were gunshots outside the house I was in. The others at the gathering were quickly on their phones and soon the room was alive with worried chatter. I went onto the roof of the building – five floors up – where I could hear more gunfire from the southern part of the town, maybe 500 metres away. Then, from the north, there was chanting and more gunshots. I went back down to my friends to find out that there had been a short demonstration in the south of the town at the stroke of midnight and the shooting from the north – a poor Alawite neighbourhood – was initiated in an attempt to frighten the protestors off the streets. The Syrian revolution had become a street versus street conflict. Hatred simmered on both sides.

***

Following the four-day lockdown of the town of Qatana in July, I stayed overnight there as soon as I could get back into the town. Qatana had experienced protests, shootings and the rumoured declaration of an Islamic emirate and an emir (or king) for the town earlier the same month. A week later the army moved in and arrested hundreds of people. Machine gun fire was heard for days right around the town as battles ensued between Sunni protestors and the military. With hundreds of soldiers and maybe a dozen tanks dug in at the four entrances to the town, protests fell silent. For a while.

With troops on the streets no one could enter or leave the town, never mind a foreigner brandishing a passport. The streets were empty, with the anti-government graffiti prominent despite already having been hurriedly painted over. Shops were still closed. During the night I was awoken by rapid-fire gun shots that ended as abruptly as it began. I stayed awake for a while, but there was not a sound from the neighbourhood, at the northern end of the town. Everyone was too fearful to move. During the lockdown, my friends who lived in the town told me they spent much of the time on the floor. Machine gun fire drilled through the air. No one went out, no one made phone calls, as the green uniformed men with machine guns (the *shabiha*) and Sunni protestors battled it out before the military succeeded in moving house to house, detaining the protestors it had previously identified from past demonstrations. The usually bustling neighbourhood that I regularly frequented, where kids would play football and adults would sit out playing backgammon, smoking *argeleh* or chatting, was dead. Most Christians in the area welcomed the army's intervention.

Even though Christians in the town were broadly uniform in their steely support for the regime, one woman's humanity overpowered her when she took in a non-Christian protestor who was being hunted by the army and security during the four-day operation. Her family pleaded with her to get the man out of the house. She wouldn't, and her family, like hundreds of others, left the town during the two hours in the morning when residents were not under curfew. She stayed and helped hide the demonstrator.

Another Christian woman told me how she brought juice out to the soldiers standing on the corner of her street. "*Haram*, they're standing there all day in the heat; it's the least I can do for them."

On 16 September a small group of men called for the fall of the regime after Friday prayers outside the town's two mosques before being dispersed by a small security force. The following Friday, I visited friends for lunch in Qatana. The protestors, buoyed by the absence of security in the town after prayers, massed in protest.

On my way out on this balmy Friday afternoon I spotted three green buses on the highway in front of me. They were filled with men in olive green military uniform, each holding an AK47. One hung out of the door, his weapon almost touching the asphalt road. Like a train, the convoy sped on towards Qatana, intent on quietening this rebellious element.

In the confusion, we were waved through the checkpoint that usually stopped us to look through my passport.

We drove straight and the three buses turned right down to an area called Ashara, before disappearing from view. Ashara is a suburb of the town that houses a large military barracks and housing for officers. The residential element of Ashara is dominated by Alawite families who have moved to the town to work with the military. They were outsiders. They arrived en masse in the town from the coast in the 1960s to keep watch over the immediate area close to the Golan Heights. Their accent differentiated them from the locals and was not even Damascene. They carried guns and held power because of this. On the streets they drove slowly through residential neighbourhoods in the dead of night, keeping watch over everyone. Most locals had loathed them ever since their arrival.

What happened in Qatana was repeated all over the country: people would protest in growing numbers, the security would photograph the protestors and take notes on the leaders. Some would be arrested and beaten by the security, and the protests would turn violent. Snipers would shoot dead the protest leaders, thereby swelling the number of anti-regime elements among the population. When a critical mass was reached the army would be called in and a short bout of fighting – usually no longer than a couple of days – would ensue. Then life would return to a tense normality among the terrorised population. Weeks or months later the people would return to the streets calling for the freedom of their relatives and friends and for the end of the Assad regime.

***

One evening during the summer of 2011, while at home, I heard an odd sound. At that time the pro-government car rallies would see a half dozen or so vehicles drive through the streets of towns and cities around Syria reminding everyone how much Bashar was loved, lest they forget.

The sound of chanting echoed over the buildings lining the town's main street and drifted in through my open window. What was strange was that there were no car horns blowing, as had always been the case with the pro-Assad rallies.

This time the sound was a little different. I could not hear the words 'Bashar' or 'Assad' from my office window being chanted. Instead I heard 'Al sh'ab, youreed ....' meaning 'the people want...' before trailing off out of earshot. I decided I needed some things from the store and walked briskly down towards the street.

When I reached the small street that led out onto the town's main thoroughfare in this largely Christian neighbourhood, there were elderly Christian women – dressed in black – staring out on to the street, thirty metres away, in complete disbelief. Some people arched their bodies to see, others looked around at each other, rendered dumb by the implausibility of what they were hearing.

"The people want the fall of the regime," over and over.

Some of the protesters held their camera phones over their heads as they walked slowly on. I could see the pictures their phones were filming. They were peaceful. They never looked left or right. They made eye contact with no one.

A short man standing on the opposite footpath looking on began to shout: "Allah, Souria, Bashar..." before being hushed down by those around him. The locals were clearly afraid.

I asked a store owner if the protestors were local. He said he didn't know.

Another store owner, from whom I went to buy cigarettes every couple of days, was talking on his mobile phone, his eyes flashing left and right while he sucked on a cigarette of his own as the group passed on into the centre of the town. This shop-keeper's wife wore no hijab. He sold alcohol. But there were no crosses hanging from his neck, or effigies of Christian figures. He must have been Alawite. So, as I watched him on his mobile phone I became convinced he was calling friends in the security or military. Sure enough, a small number of people arrived thirty minutes after the protestors had passed and gathered next to his shop. It was a pathetic effort. There were three men dressed in military fatigues and maybe ten in civilian clothing. They shouted slogans of support for Bashar, but by then the shock had been inflicted on the locals.

I remember thinking the protesters were incredibly brave. But I was more drawn to what was now facing the locals, who had their normalcy destroyed in a matter of a few minutes. On their shocked faces a whole new reality was unfolding before their eyes. They had been watching the protest movement from television screens or listening to stories of revolt for months, but now it was in their streets, their neighbourhood. The time was coming for them – whether they wanted or not – to pick sides.

On a cold January night I went for *shawarma* sandwiches. It was about ten minutes before 10pm. My thoughts were preoccupied by how the town would look as it descended into darkness from the power cut (up to seven hours a day at that point) at ten o'clock amongst the newly-erected sandbag barriers around the main police station, where men in civilian clothing carried guns. I pulled up outside the *shawarma* restaurant in the centre of the town and sat in the car. In seconds a crowd swept up fifty metres in front of me. It could only be one thing. A huge free Syria flag was unfurled. It was the green of the flag that caught my eye and held my stare. The combined sound of the protestors boomed through the streets, "God is greatest, freedom, God is greatest, freedom," they cried. They were incredibly energised, incredibly motivated. They stood at the crossroads chanting and jumping for about five minutes. The huge flag meant no traffic could pass and an old man directed cars down a side street and away from the ecstatic crowd, though it appeared he had nothing to do with the protest. Others cowered in their cars; some scampered to put their groceries into the back seats.

At this point I became aware that the police station was not far behind me. Fear crept up my spine as I realised bullets could pass over my head at any second. But it never happened. A security car passed within inches of the outermost protestors but continued on down the street. The man behind the cash register at the restaurant said it happened quite often here in this, a town that rarely made headlines for dissent. There were several customers in the restaurant who were not bothered to get up from their seats to see what was going on. Others stood in the street looking on. Were they against the protestors? Perhaps they would have liked to take part but were afraid? Neither the police nor the security services attacked these demonstrators. They did not even come to look. It was, I thought at the time, how freedom should be. If only the rest of Syria could have experienced such restraint. Later, I spoke to my local shopkeeper, a Sunni, about the emerging protests in the town. "You need to watch Tom and Jerry on television, then you will understand the game being played here."

***

Travelling widely around the country was an impossibility – it just couldn't have been done, or rather, I could have visited other major cities, but I would have been found, detained and deported from the country like so many other reporters, and there would have been no book or other reports. Being one of a handful of reporters based permanently in the country during the uprising, I believed it to be more important to remain out of sight, even if it meant I could not regularly file from the scene of arrests and shootings of protestors, or meet the Free Syria Army. As recorded in these pages, I did witness the anger of protesters calling for the downfall of the regime; I did see the security services beat and detain peaceful student protestors in the heart of Damascus. But organising with activists to visit protest spots was usually a risk too great. It was clearly possible to experience the anger of the street first-hand, but not by involving activists in such plans.

The journalist Omar al-Assad, who contributed to the pan-Arab daily *Al-Hayat* and the Lebanese daily *As-Safir*, was arrested by Syrian security forces on 3 July in Qaddam after attending the funeral of a protestor. Amer Matar, a journalist for *Al-Hayat*, was another taken from the streets in early September. He stood before the Fourth Magistrate Judge on 8 December and denied charges of "weakening national morale" before being sent back to the infamous Adra prison north of Damascus. Any journalist who thought they were not under constant surveillance during the unrest was, at best, naïve, and at worst dumb. On 29 October I heard my former colleague and friend, Lina Ibrahim, had been kidnapped in Harasta, where she lived with her father. At the time, Harasta was experiencing nightly anti-regime demonstrations because security forces were shooting and detaining locals. Lina, a journalist who pursued business stories out of her fear of writing about politics, wrote for Bloomberg. We had worked together at *Syria Times* in 2007 and 2008. She was released on 17 November, following an announcement by the regime that it would set free 1,184 "political detainees". The same day the Free Syria Army launched the boldest attack to date on a complex which housed the air force security in Harasta. The FSA used rocket-propelled grenades and machine gun fire. Eight people were reportedly killed. In December, I visited the Ministry for Information to apply to visit Homs or Hama with the government. "Yes, we can organise this, you can meet the governor of Hama, but Homs is too dangerous, we cannot go there," said the Ministry employee. I waited a few days and called. They said they were still waiting to get clearance from the minister. Each week for a month I continued to call, but the problem now was that they had to wait for a group of journalists to go, they could not take me alone. By January 2012, the indiscriminate violence – clear from YouTube clips purportedly taken around the country – became widespread. Friends pleaded with me not to pursue the trip. One wet January night I watched a video supposedly showing a convoy of security forces driving along a country road in Deraa province. Metres in front of the camera a group of men with AK47s leaned over the roof of a building and began to open fire wildly on the convoy. The first jeep and minibus slowly came to a halt. The jeep at the back of the convoy attempted to back up but also stopped slowly. The fire from the roof-top rebels was ferocious.

The thought that there could have been anyone in the convoy shook me. The bus could have contained ordinary civilians, journalists, government workers or even the Arab League observers. For a period my appetite to visit Hama with the Ministry officials died. But images on state television of Asian journalists and photographers trooping around after the Arab League observers was too much for me to take. On 10 January I called the Ministry for Information again. "These journalists are here in Syria for only a few days but you are here long-term so you don't qualify," said the assistant to the foreign media director when I asked for my name to be put down for a journalists' trip to Homs the following day. "Am I going to be granted permission to travel on another occasion?" I asked. "We'll see," she said.

The next afternoon news broke on Twitter that foreign journalists had been killed in Homs. An award-winning French cameraman, Gilles Jacquier, was fatally injured when a mortar landed close to him in a pro-regime neighbourhood of the city. A Dutch journalist was also badly injured. Again my appetite to travel had been quickly, eerily sated. But only for a while.

***

In June 2011, I made yet another visit to the Ministry for Information on the eighth floor of the Baath newspaper building. On this occasion I was looking for a document that would allow me back into Syria if I wanted to leave. I knocked on one of two offices that dealt with the foreign journalist contingent. No one answered and I walked in. There were four employees sitting on sofas talking, drinking tea and *mette* and smoking.

I called over to an employee I knew.

"Hello, Basil."

"Oh, hi Stephen, how are you?" asked Basil, who asked me about English grammar each time I visited. He was chatting on the internet and playing games. The darkened windows were open and the sound of traffic from the Mezzah highway below floated up into the room.

He went out to ask another employee about my request, then returned and asked if I wanted some tea. I did. As I waited for the employee to arrive I spotted some newspapers piled up on a chair. I looked through them: the *Wall Street Journal*, *The Guardian*, the *International Herald Tribune*, the *Financial Times*, *The Times*, the *Sunday Telegraph*.

The employee emerged and told me what I need to bring: a letter saying I would be leaving and specifying when I would return, including my journalist details. Basil returned with the tea, and we sat there smoking. "Is there any chance I could take some of these newspapers?" I asked.

"Yes, go ahead," he replied. I'm delighted to have scooped these rare sources of information. They are not easily found and if one can find them, each can cost about US$5 in Damascus – a hefty price.

Among the bunch, *The Guardian* had been opened and folded back to the world news pages. I looked down to see an article on Syria with one of the paragraphs underlined in blue pen ink. The paragraph stated how Syrian security forces had been shooting and torturing peaceful protestors.

In a department where few worked and fewer appeared to take their work seriously, these employees were reading the foreign press. They were keeping tabs on what was being said about the regime. They were reading the above-mentioned publications – the ones they could get their hands on – and were highlighting the parts they found disagreeable.

Generalisations have been sweeping in the international and national debate on the Syrian uprising. Some Alawites I know were fervently anti-regime. Some Sunnis would die for the president. Similarly, some of the government employees I dealt with went out of their way to be unhelpful, but others were quite the opposite.

In mid-September I went to the *Hijra wa Jawazat* (passport department) in Rukn Eldeen in north Damascus. I had been there several times before. One police officer even stopped me in the corridor to say hello and ask how I'd been.

The men here work under very difficult circumstances. They must spend hours searching through reams of papers looking for information about this or that Iraqi refugee. They must deal with the hundreds of arms that hang over their heads, mostly belonging to Iraqi refugees, those looking to find out if they must leave the country or are allowed to stay on in their new home, Syria.

They are all polite. One man granted me the all-important stamp allowing me to stay a month longer – without having to go back to the Ministry for Information for permission as I probably should have – because he knew me.

These were not the men who drive the Hummers, the Mercedes or the BMWs. They were more likely the people who drove taxis after work, searching out passengers on the streets of the capital until well after dark in order to make ends meet.

***

Whether civil war takes hold of Syria or not, it will be down to the people – not Bashar al-Assad or the opposition organisations. One evening in September I took a public microbus home from Damascus. The previous day a twelve-year-old boy had been shot dead in Kisweh, south of Damascus, on the first day of the new school year. On the route was a housing complex built for police officers and their families. (The socialist idea is to build homes for many public workers.) At the entrance to the housing complex is an arch. When someone wants to alert the driver to let them off the micro they regularly say "let me down" or simply "the corner" or "the tunnel". Similarly, when someone wants to get off the micro at the police housing complex they often say "the arch", meaning the entrance to the housing project. People from Damascus and many of the towns and villages down to Deraa and north to Homs do not pronounce the letter *qaf* in Arabic, whereas Syrians from the coastal region do; it is something unmistakable. The letter *qaf* is the first in the Arabic word for arch. So when a man asked the driver to let him down at the *qos*, or arch, instead of the *os* as it is commonly called in southern parts of the country, immediately the other passengers in the micro knew that the man to whom the voice belonged was from the coast. Minds raced, putting two and two together, adding the fact that he was getting down from the micro at the police housing complex. This could only mean he was an Alawite and probably worked with the security forces or the police.

Whether he was a security policeman or a traffic guard or simply visiting, he held a position of power over those in the micro. He was in all likelihood oblivious to what it meant to use the letter *qaf*. To the other passengers he was probably responsible for spying on or beating protestors. He was at least responsible for promoting the new culture of fear. During these times of fear and unrest Syrians quite naturally held on tightest to the aspects of life they knew and trusted most: family, neighbours, clan. Pronouncing this letter made him different: a policeman, a security agent, or simply Alawite. In a majority Sunni country, he was the other and he represented the regime, a regime many held responsible for the deaths of thousands around the country.

***

When the Damascus branch of the Baath party in Mazraah was targeted in an RPG (rocket-propelled grenade) attack on 20 November – the first such incident inside the capital – activists claimed responsibility for it. The following day, however, Colonel Riad al-Asaad, the head of the so-called Free Syria Army, denied responsibility for the attack.

But it was on the morning of 23 December that twenty-three Damascenes finally experienced what some had been waiting for, and what all were dreading. Syrian state television and Dunia, the pro-regime station, broadcast a scene of utter mayhem outside a major security facility close to Kafr Souseh square: blackened bodies still sitting in the shell of a car, human entrails cast across broken concrete, brain matter and bones, all added to a sickening scene. Remarkable for a regime forged in nebulosity, within ten minutes cameras belonging to these broadcasters had reached the bomb site. Shortly after, Al Qaeda was blamed by regime mouthpieces for the attacks. It was the morning after the first group of Arab League monitors arrived in Damascus. Only the previous night I had driven past one of the security buildings targeted and remarked to myself how it would make a fine target for someone wanting to send a serious message to the regime. I thought how such a move would strike fear into the government.

Covering the incident for *The Times*, I was quickly on my way to the scene.

The streets and roads around Damascus were surprisingly busy. On previous Fridays, the chief day of protest and consequent crackdown, such highways were deserted. Most feared venturing out and, for me, driving into the city was always an unnerving experience because the roads were devoid of the bustling life I had long been accustomed to. This time, however, the cars around me provided a form of comfort. Half a dozen United Nations vans and ambulances rushed towards the capital from the Golan Heights, weaving carefully through light traffic. After taking several detours through the less developed parts of Kafr Souseh in order to avoid security checkpoints, I got as far as Kafr Souseh square, about one hundred metres from the scene of one of the explosions. A roadblock manned by police men denied immediate entry to the section of street blown up and there was no way of entering the bomb site. Water from fire trucks flooded the street next to the mangled and levelled walls. The entire open facade of the complex had disappeared as a result of the blast. The second bombing, about a kilometre west of the first, took place at another security building close to Jumarek square. All streets in this area were swiftly closed down and I could not get a clear sight of the scene there. Thereafter, the streets around this military intelligence complex were indefinitely blocked off. For the first time checkpoints had been erected inside the city centre. Anti-suicide blast walls sprung up around all major security and military facilities in the city. Nervous men dressed in civilian clothing stared out at passing traffic. In the eyes of many in Midan, Baramkeh and Kafr Souseh, Baghdad had arrived in Damascus.

The regime, so opaque in addressing issues of internal security, immediately blamed Al Qaeda, an organisation that almost always claimed responsibility for its work. In the days and weeks that followed, military and security facilities both inside the capital and in the suburbs used concrete blocks, metal rods and whatever could be found to hastily make makeshift, ridiculous looking military posts and, thus, build even greater physical and figurative divisions between the people and the authorities. In practice these additions would have done little to decrease the effects of an attack by rebel forces, imagined or otherwise. But they did succeed in striking further fear into the civilian populations that drove past each every day and were caught up in traffic for hours where they had never been before. At Kafr Souseh square concrete barriers were laid out on the street in left and right formation to slow traffic speed and prevent car bombers breaching the facilities' walls, something I had not seen since my travels in northern Iraq in 2008.

During the funeral ceremonies the following day, an imam cast blame for the bombings on the opposition leader, Burhan Ghalioun, from the pulpit of the Omayyed mosque. The mourners were dominated by security operatives and the crowd outside the mosque waved flags bearing the face of the president. The funerals were clearly hijacked by the regime. The names and identities of the dead were never distinguished. What the regime's media tools did not report was the pitiful attendance at a pro-government rally at Sabah Baharet in central Damascus that Friday evening. It had been planned since at least the night before – during a drive past the square twenty-four hours previously, I saw men constructing a stage in front of the Central Bank of Syria. But very few turned out.

Responsibility for the 23 December, 6 January, 17 March and 10 May bombings in Damascus and for another at a military complex in Aleppo on 10 February was uncertain. American officials blamed Al Qaeda, as did the Syrian authorities. Residents of Midan thought differently. A businessman from this restive district told me shortly after the December bombings that the streets around the compound were closed "for four hours that morning". Another woman who worked at a recording studio and who lived next to the Kafr Souseh intelligence building said helicopters had been flying overhead earlier on the morning of 6 January. She said locals were not allowed outside. "When we heard the bomb blast we were eating breakfast, but none of us were surprised – we expected something to happen."

***

When the foreign editor of *The Times* in London, Richard Beeston, contacted me to say he was coming to Syria I felt pressure fall upon me. By then, late January, several journalists had been allowed to enter the country, perhaps because the regime felt the situation on the ground would support their longstanding claims that it was battling armed gangs. The drive to get out and see things for myself was overwhelming.

My quandary was that I was attempting to compete with journalists coming to Syria for a week or two while I had been living here for years. Unquestionably, my experience, knowledge and language skills were important advantages in understanding and reporting the revolt. But a very different set of consequences that applied to my case clearly did not apply to the wave of journalists that descended on Syria in January 2012 and flew off days later.

Weeks of hounding the Syrian Ministry for Information officials for permission to accompany the Arab League monitors proved fruitless. So on the evening of 27 January I visited the Sheraton hotel in Damascus to ask about the Arab League observers' next planned trip. The lobby was dotted with state security men, loitering around or sitting on the numerous sofas, smoking. I was directed into an office where four men − unmistakably Syrian − sat around sheets of paper. They looked busy and were probably planning how to deceive the observers in their next mission. Looking me up and down they told me to go back out and ask at the reception for the Arab League representative. Outside, Ghaleb Saad, a Jordanian, was sitting and talking with another man. I introduced myself, telling him I had been in Syria for several years. He walked me out of the lobby and into a restaurant at the back of the hotel, clearly to avoid the ears of the *mukhabarat*.

"I need something from you," he said. "As you know, one of our four mandates is to assess how journalists are being allowed to operate in Syria. How do you find it working here?" I told him that I first wanted some sort of guarantee that I would accompany the observers on any trip the next day. Saad called Jaafar Kibeida, one of the mission's leaders, and relayed to me that it would be no problem. I then told Saad that nothing extraordinary had happened to me personally, largely, I thought, because I was being extremely careful. "I don't speak to anyone out of the ordinary. I try to keep a routine. But I do know journalists who have been detained for weeks and months without charge," I told him. He asked me to write some kind of report about how life is working as a journalist − which I never did since the mission was cancelled for security reasons the following day. He said, away from the security officers, that they were planning to visit Harasta and "maybe Douma" the next morning. As I left the hotel grounds I spied the smashed observer jeep somehow driven down from Lattakia and stashed away in a corner of the Sheraton hotel's car park.

And so, at 9am the next morning, 28 January, I returned to the hotel.

A small number of journalists stumbled out of the elevator to the restaurant for breakfast. I approached one observer to ask when, where and if the mission was going anywhere today. He said there might be a trip but he was not sure. I chatted to Jon Lee Anderson of *The New Yorker* for a moment as he ate breakfast. He was of the opinion that the government-organised tours were a joke, but a trip to Saqba east of Damascus the day before had been enlightening.

I went back out to the lobby to try to get some more information. "One of the vehicles has a flat tyre," Kibeida told me. "But we are planning to go somewhere soon with a couple of the observers."

In the end I found out the destination from one of the burly Syrian security men guarding the mission Mercedes outside the hotel's main door. "They're going to Rankous," he said.

Almost an hour's drive north of Damascus between the snow-covered Christian towns of Saidnaya and Maaloula, the farming hamlet of Rankous had been boiling in anti-regime dissent for months. Close to the Lebanese border, locals were able to smuggle in small arms to defend themselves and their demonstrators from the Syrian army. On this Saturday morning, the town had been out of the regime's control for almost a week.

By now I had my own car and chose, with much trepidation, to drive out to Rankous with the observers' convoy. The forty-five-minute drive was perhaps the most dangerous episode of the trip. Just outside Damascus, close to the restive suburb of Berzah, two Syrian television minibuses crashed into each other just behind me. For me, it was imperative that I keep up with the convoy in order to be admitted to the scene. We drove on, up through the hills north of the capital. From a window several stories up in the town of Al Tal, a centre of protest in the summer of 2011, came a shout directed at our quickly passing convoy.

There was snow on the road approaching Saidnaya. We drove past the roundabout leading up to the town and continued straight. Soldiers guarding checkpoints and locals alike looked on in amazement. Ten minutes later the convoy slowed down as we arrived at another roundabout. Here maybe two dozen soldiers could be seen. They ran to prepare themselves as the cars pull up. Out into the freezing wind we disembarked. The Syrian television crews were quickly at work filming the observers walking around the square where soldiers looked on. The security officers sent to protect the observers looked very nervous indeed. There was no sign of Anderson or the *New York Times* reporters. A strange silence hung in the mountain air.

The observers were taken to the side of the checkpoint on the square and shown what appeared to be bullets holes in sandbags shielding a military post. "This happened last night at about 11pm," said a fearful young soldier stationed inside the snow-covered checkpoint. "They drove down to the edge of the checkpoint and started shooting. Then they drove off."

I asked him what kind of car they were driving and how many gunmen there were. He looked nervous. He did not answer my questions.

A microbus carrying a handful of passengers stopped at the checkpoint and the TV cameras grouped round like hyenas frenzying on a kill. The passengers, a couple of young men, were dazed. Of course, they could read the word 'Dunia' written on the microphone, and so they knew what they ought and ought not to say.

Security officers stopped a truck and ordered the driver to get down – it is difficult to differentiate between the regular soldiers and the security, I remarked to myself.

"We are here to help you and to listen to you," Kibeida told the truck driver as the television cameras huddled around.

Then a taxi approached the checkpoint but did not stop – the single most menacing thing I saw that cold January day was the gaze of a security officer directed towards this taxi driver.

One observer walked unnoticed in the direction of Rankous to a small house on the side of the road. A man appeared at the gate of a house and the cameras rushed towards him as he and the observer chatted. "We are one people; we are not interested in politics here. We just want a simple, safe life," he said.

When I walked past him fifteen minutes later, he had a boy at his side, and – his face told a different story as he looked at me – a knowing, forlorn smile.

The observers asked to drive on into Rankous and their driver was sought, and found, but refused to go in – it was too dangerous, he said. The observers were stuck.

A security officer walked with me up the hill in the direction of Rankous, two kilometres away. "There are only a few families left there, most have left because of the gangs," he said. "We don't control the town anymore, the gangs do," he added, completely sure of his assertion.

"You see, the border is just over those mountains and they can get anything they can from Lebanon; we can't control the whole border."

For the clamouring Syrian journalists the event had never been serious. They laughed and joked, shooting the same scenes over and over. There were no questions for the observers; there was never a hint of seriousness, one that could reflect the state of their own country.

Jaafar Kibeida turned to me and said: "What do you think?" in English. Immediately the Syrian television crew swarmed around and listened to me return a question back at him – I didn't want to publicly give my opinion which might have placed people I knew in danger. I later asked one of the presenters not to broadcast the short interview for the benefit of my Syrian friends and contacts.

About thirty minutes later, two middle-aged army officers arrived at the fortified roundabout. The foreign journalists had also just arrived.

"You can go in; you are free to go into Rankous, but in my opinion, it's not a good idea," one of the officers told the observers. Still, the observers had no driver.

The three observers walked back up the hill and gazed into Rankous below before turning back to the square. They got into their Mercedes and sped back down the mountains through melting snow to Damascus. They had essentially seen nothing, or nothing that could illustrate a peaceful uprising. It was the mission's final day of operations in Syria; I had been lucky.

I certainly didn't feel lucky when Jon Lee Anderson, who was also with the tour, posted pictures of Free Syria Army rebels from the same town a couple of hours later on Twitter. I was, in fact, devastated, but motivated.

Had I stayed with the *New York Times* reporters and Anderson I would have surely continued on to meet the rebels. The journalists were meeting the insurgents as tanks surrounded the town and gunfire flew overhead later the same afternoon. But coming back down the hill that led out of Rankous, next to the three chicken huts, I would have passed maybe two dozen soldiers and security officers, as well as tanks, before getting into my easily identifiable car. I was not on assignment – I was still living in the same country that was my home. I would drive thirty kilometres, buy my litre of milk and go home, not to a hotel. And I would certainly be identified and forced to leave the country, or worse.

The next day I met Ahmad, a factory worker, in Damascus. He was studying for the IELTS English-language exam as he hoped to emigrate to Canada within a year. He told me his brother-in-law was killed the previous week in Rankous by the army. His relative was, he said, a member of the Free Syria Army. "If they can hold out then the regime will fall within two weeks, *Inshallah*," he said. The pounding of Rankous continued in the hours after the observers left for several days, and the rebels fled over the Lebanese border the same day the Syrian army regained control of the towns outside eastern Damascus that had fallen out of the regime's control. It would be much more than two weeks before Ahmad's dreams would be realised.

***

A couple of days later I met up with Beeston and his photographer. I surely betrayed envy as I listen to their stories from Zabadani, Deraa and Saqba. They were planning to go back to Saqba, east of Damascus, the next day to seek out an underground field hospital. Beeston asked if I wanted to come. I asked him in return if they had contacts there and if they had a car and driver organised. He told me they had no contacts but the car and driver were ready. I could not turn down the invite.

The following morning at 10am I waited outside the Ministry for Information for Beeston, his photographer and a Spanish journalist.

The previous Friday a team of foreign journalists that included reporters from RT, the BBC, the *Washington Post*, *The New York Times*, Jon Lee Anderson and Beeston had entered the eastern Damascus suburb of Saqba to be greeted by a sight that did not bode well for the Syrian regime. About 5,000 demonstrators gathered after a funeral and called for the fall of the regime. They were protected by groups of fighters from the Free Syria Army. One female journalist was hoisted on protestors' shoulders. Victory, it seemed, was nigh – several other neighbourhoods nearby saw rebels set up checkpoints and essentially take control. The area, along with Douma, Arbeen and Hamourieh, all long protest hubs, were free.

We got into the taxi and headed across the city towards Saqba, a working-class suburb just east of the Damascus ring road. We passed Jaramanah driving north and encountered a large puddle and several soldiers stopping traffic entering and exiting the side road into Saqba. Our driver told one of the soldiers we were foreign journalists. He looked in and waved us on. The same incident took place a further three times. The soldiers had yellow plastic ribbons tied to their jacket lapels to indicate they were regime forces, not rebels. Driving deeper into the district there were few signs of life, though a queue of people waiting for bread outside a bakery told us there were residents here. Parked next to them were an ambulance, a military jeep and an armoured vehicle painted blue and bearing the word POLICE on its sides. The ambulance and jeep were normal sights for me, but the blue armoured vehicle was not. Further ahead on the street were three green buses, the type I saw used to transport soldiers to Qatana the previous summer. By now, there was no mobile phone coverage – the authorities had cut the network. We were in the hands of the army and the dissenting locals – sworn enemies – should anything happen to us. Two men stared with open mouths as a truck laden down with gas canisters entered the area in front of us – they were surprised they now had gas with which to cook. Saqba was not how it was the previous week: it was clearly a fresh war zone. Machine gun bullet holes were visible on the top floors of several buildings both to our left and our right. In one, a hole about a foot in diameter was surrounded by gunfire pockmarks. There must have been anti-regime elements inside. A government sniper appeared on top of one building next to a satellite dish surveying all. Further on towards the centre of Saqba I spotted on a low street wall the green, white and black of the free Syria flag roughly painted. The army had not had the opportunity to paint over this notorious symbol of dissent, though it still amazed me to see that it had not been erased.

We continued on in search of the square – Municipal Square – where the 5,000 anti-regime protestors gathered with such hope only days before, and where we hoped to find the underground hospital.

We arrived at the square and were met by a scene of devastation. The whole sides of houses had caved in, exposing the everyday household items within. Curtains, electric heaters, painted walls, pictures still hanging. An electricity pole was smashed in half close to the ground, splinters spiking high into the air. Only a tank shell, fired low, could have caused such damage. The monument in the centre of the square was now rubble. Several local men came close and held up a large shell casing for us to see. They were incredulous as to what had happened in their own neighbourhood. Other men appeared in the corner of the square behind a barricade of rubbish bins. They stared over at us but did not approach. After an observably vicious fight, Saqba was back in the hands of the regime.

Beeston and I walked to the opposite corner of the square where there are three men signalling to us to come close. "They arrived Saturday and blew us away. There were Hezbollah soldiers with them," said one man. When prompted about how he knew the nationality of the soldiers he said he knew because he recognised their accents. He said the attack stopped just this morning. I'm speaking Arabic and I'm very aware they might identify me as being Syrian because of my Damascus accent. Perhaps there are regime sympathisers among them. I made it clear to them I'm from another country.

"Come see the mosque," one said and we followed him across to the opposite side of the square. The local men were incredibly brave – to be seen guiding foreign journalists through this built up area would mean severe repercussions for them. The army were close by, though we couldn't see them now. Machine gun fire rang around in the air. We were taken to a mosque just off the square. I walked past without noticing it but was told to look up. A gaping hole had been blasted in the side of the mosque's minaret. I asked if the rebels were inside the mosque. "There was no one there – if they [the rebels] were inside they would have been at the top," said one man. The hole was about two feet wide and located half way down the minaret. It was a desecration of a religious site and, as such, a war crime.

A man carrying a bag of fruit whistled to get my attention and knowingly nodded at me, indicating to follow him. I hesitate, more concerned with the crowds of men quickly forming around us. They were telling their stories to me but I warned them to disperse for their own good. Military vehicles were close by, outside the recently recaptured police station we had seen on our way to the square. More machine gun fire crackled in the air. It was cold; several angry men asked if we were from Russia and pointed up at the mosque.

The streets were almost empty. My shoes moved over a carpet of glass and rubble. Pieces of metal covered the wet concrete. "Do you want to see the bodies?" the man holding the bags of fruit asked. He told me that over the previous few days people had had to bury their family members in their gardens and in the earth outside their homes. Fear gripped me – the area was clearly under government control again and there might have been snipers looking out for any remnants of the rebels, or simply employed to subvert a local population perhaps buoyed by the presence of journalists. We walked away from the square and crossed an open street running. An old man wandered out of a destroyed shop gazing at us. We then walked briskly in single file down a side street and through narrow passages dividing houses. Water dripped into a shallow puddle and I hopped around it. After about a hundred metres we came to a clearing and the man guiding us called to another now close by. "Do you have the keys?" he asked a second man we had not seen before. He then shouted at another man staring out of his house door, gesticulating for him to go back inside. The man came with the keys and opened the large metal door that appeared to me to be the entrance to a hospital. There were now no buildings in front of us, just open sky. The complex was, in fact, a school, long closed down. In the corner to the right of the door were half a dozen pine trees. Under them were uneven lumps in the ground. Another man joined us and began peeling back the now apparent plastic sheeting covered over by branches, carpets and pine leaves.

It was difficult to look at the disfigured, swollen faces. One body had its eyes gouged out and part of its face missing. Another closest to the school building wall was blackened. "They killed him as he was lighting a fire in his house. Then they threw him into it," said one of our guides. They must have been killed on the previous Friday or Saturday. Their flesh had turned a bluish colour and the bodies had swollen. The top row of teeth of one man gaped out through his missing lips. Another had a white bandage across his waist. It appeared he was not killed outright and attempts were made to save his life.

"There are six men here and they were all killed in the last few days," said one of the men.

"We are hiding them here so that we can bury them ourselves. If we go to a hospital they [the security] will take them and we won't even get a burial. They already took one body," he added, anger and bewilderment deep in his voice. I asked the men if the dead were fighters or soldiers. "They are civilians," one replied.

There was no real smell – it was too cold. Their hands were bound as is the tradition with the dead here in order to avoid the effects of rigor mortis. The expressions on their dead faces reflected the millisecond of fear, shock and pain going through their minds as life left their bodies, each one different

Photos were taken and questions asked. There were several other sites where locals were holding their dead relatives in a state of limbo, they said. The men were not afraid; it seemed they were living in an alternative reality. Staring death in the face, be it through martyred friends and neighbours or through the regime's tanks and machine guns, had become the norm for them. "People are burying their dead under their houses – there is nowhere else to take them," said one man. The impulse to keep moving grew inside me with each minute we spent there. I began to get edgy and after about ten minutes we left the communal grave. If the army or security found us we were likely to be shot too. We were now witnesses to the regime's death squads. The mutilation of the bodies, the gouged out eyes, amounted to war crimes.

We stole back in the direction of the square and to our waiting car. On the way I walked over more glass and mangled metal, cracking under my body weight. Shops without window fronts. Televisions exposed to the rain. There were no people in these destroyed homes.

We jumped back into the car where our driver was waiting for us, remarkably calm.

"Who will pay for all of this?" said a young man, pointing at the destroyed and mangled buildings around us in through the car window. "Will the Free Army? Will Bashar's army? No, we will pay. I hate the Free Army – they brought death and destruction to our homes and now they are gone leaving us here with the regime soldiers," he added. I asked him to clarify what he meant as all the residents we had spoken to said the regime's army was responsible for the destruction and deaths.

"When the army comes and they see people on the streets with guns and who are shooting of course they will try to kill them. They think this is their job. They think they [the armed men] are terrorists."

Suddenly a government convoy rolled by our car and through the square. APVs were painted blue to give the idea they were police and not military vehicles. In a thirty-two-seater bus were dozens of soldiers, guns resting on their laps. The young man crouched next to the car out of their view. We were incredibly lucky to be back in the vehicle. When we talked to locals the army was nowhere to be seen. We managed to visit the bodies without being detected. It was only when we returned to the relative safety of the car that they appeared on the streets, the Saqba residents looking on helplessly.

On the way out we were stopped at each checkpoint again and at one a soldier slipped his hand in through the front passenger window and opened the glove compartment of the car while talking casually to us. When he found nothing he let us go. The soldier guarding the next was Alawite, said our driver, able to tell from his accent. "Come over here and see what the fighters did here," he urged us, foaming at the mouth. We declined, keen to get out of this fresh and bloody war zone. The bizarreness of returning to the city centre fifteen minutes from Saqba, where life continued in apparent normalcy, was astounding.

The men I met in Saqba were not freedom fighters, they were not political. But the death and violence brought on by Syria's emerging civil conflict tied them up in a struggle between life and death. The ideas of freedom and hope have long passed from their thoughts. For them to even be seen talking to jour-nalists would in all likelihood mean a painful end for them. The other districts east of the capital, celebrated by many as centres newly freed from Assad's rule the previous week, fell the same way as Saqba.

The blood of Syrians is expensive, they shouted, at both pro- and anti-regime gatherings. In Saqba, however, blood was as ex-pendable as the drops of rain that fell out of the sky that cold day; lives cheap; homes worthless. The will of the strong had been imposed once more. The Syrian regime would not give up without a fight, evidently, to the death, and when its soldiers and security officers saw men with guns the propaganda that told of armed gangs rang true for them.

The men who uncovered the six bodies linger long in my mind. What then for them? What did they think of having to take care of the dead? Dead men they did not know. How would they go on in the knowledge that the Syrian army was back? Having tasted, smelt and lived death, were they no longer afraid to die? For Syria? For Sabqa? For their sons and daughters? For 'freedom'?

And what about the dead men? Surely they had brothers, sons, cousins, friends, who from the day of death will never, ever forgive the regime, will never agree to allowing it to rule over Syria, who would fight, protest and probably kill for an idea that borders between revenge and freedom.

**

With the withdrawal of the Arab League monitors and many foreign journalists in early February, Syrians were once again on their own. Tanks and checkpoints returned to several other towns around the capital, including Qatana to the south west. At the time, locals feared the army was gearing up for more assaults, something it could do uninterrupted and out of sight of the outside world. I had spoken to a number of foreign journalists in Syria on temporary visas and all said their time was up in the first week of February but they hoped to have them renewed.

Two days later, with the Arab League observers gone and the journalists out of the country, the Syrian regime laid waste to Homs. At around 8pm on Friday, 3 February – two days after my trip to Saqba and seven after the announcement of the end of the Arab League mission – shells began landing on the Khalediya and Baba Amr areas of Homs. It did not stop for four hours. Hundreds were reported to have died, many when their own homes fell on them. By Monday, 6 February, perhaps 400 shells and rockets had fallen on Bab Amr from army positions outside the city. Hundreds were killed as shells continued to fall for weeks. It was the most devastating operation against dissenting elements in eleven months of revolt. The same day the American embassy in Damascus closed, pulling its entire staff from the country. Activists reported dozens of APVs and tanks gathering around the town of Zabadani which had, until then, been free from government control for several weeks. It fell to regime forces on 10 February when the Free Syria Army fled further up the mountains and on into Lebanon. The residents remained. The BBC, *Washington Post* and other foreign journalists who had managed to enter Zabadani were long gone. The images they broadcast to millions around the world similarly forgotten.

During early February I began hearing gunshots and explosions from my house at night. In Qatana, a fifteen minute drive, the army had cut off outside access to the town. In the opposite direction to the east, the town of Madamiyeh was subjected to several security operations. Slightly further south, twenty-one people were killed the previous Saturday, 4 February when the security broke up a demonstration/funeral in Dariya. A friend living there in the town said the town was also cut off from the outside world. The country was falling apart as the regime imposed its will like never before. Past whispers of war were now fact.

VIII

HISTORY, BLAME AND RESPONSIBILITY

In October 2008 a colleague at *Syria Times*, who part-timed as
a fixer for international journalists, called me aside to tell me
about the sentencing of a group of human rights activists and
lawyers on trial for speaking out against the state. The sentencing was to take place in a couple of days and I needed to find
an outlet for the story. The fixer could set up interviews with
human rights lawyers – for a hefty price of US$100 – but I had
secured Asia Times Online to cover the story.

The National Security Court building, located close to the entrance of the bustling Souk Hamadiyeh in downtown Damascus,
is one of the busiest public institutions in the country.

Mothers and other relatives spend hours waiting and hoping
to hear news of sons and husbands arrested or detained. Lawyers scamper between the families and the legal authorities
seeking information and attempting to calm relatives. Students
of law carry documents from office to office inside the court
building looking for stamps and signatures. Streams of people
stand around outside on the street as police vans pass in and out
through a gate to the left of the court. Tourists pass by, unaware
of what goes on inside.

On this particular Wednesday in October a large crowd had
gathered just inside the National Security Court. The group of
twelve human rights activists included Anwar al-Bunni, Riad Seif
and Michel Kilo. I had brought my camera and a Danish friend.
We squeezed through the crowds up to the first floor court room
where the sentencing would take place. There was hardly a
breath of air in the room, which was filled with family members,

a scattering of journalists and representatives from the Danish, Canadian and Dutch embassies. My Danish friend had to leave early on the verge of passing out from a lack of oxygen, before the court sat. The accused stood at the right in the court room inside a large metal cage. Looking jaded, but happy, they waved to family members and blew kisses. They appeared as if they had forgotten where they were, taking in the joy of seeing their loved ones. Silence fell as the judge entered. In the space of a few seconds, the eleven men and one woman were sentenced to two-and-a-half years in prison. The sentenced stood up and waved 'V' signs with their fingers. The foreign diplomats looked utterly afraid and entirely out of place amid the shouting and heat. After the judge had left the twelve continued to shout and blow kisses at their friends and relatives. They appeared as if they had not heard the judge's words. It seemed they did not care. They were using this opportunity instead to see their families, the new nieces and nephews. They didn't know when they would have the chance again. Then they were taken away.

The spirit of revolution in Syria was not born in March 2011 or even in that claustrophobic Damascus courtroom in the autumn of 2008. Indeed, as in many colonised territories and states that have had foreign control imposed on them, the twentieth century was one of turbulence and change for Syria. What concerns us in the murky half-light between revolt and potential civil war in 2012 is how past uprisings may point to an outcome between two seemingly immovable agents.

When the French bombed Damascus in October 1925, Muslim *qabadayat* or quarter youth gang leaders went to the Christian and Jewish quarters located in the east and south east of the Old City to protect locals from any possible marauding gangs that might take advantage of the strife. Islamic slogans, God is greatest, were chanted by the revolutionaries, as was the case in 2011, but the leading revolutionary figures saw an importance in protecting these minorities.

At that time, "Damascus' nationalist leadership had not inspired or led the uprising. The city's traditional notable leadership and the members of its great families disavowed any role or responsibility for the uprising and were concerned with ensuring the security of their property against marauding rioters and later from the French bombardment," wrote Michael Provence in *The Great Syrian Revolt and the Rise of Arab Nationalism*.

In 2011 the city dwellers of Aleppo and Damascus made up the overwhelming majority of the 'silent majority'; those who hated the regime for what it was doing to fellow Syrians, but did not feel motivated enough to do anything about it.

According to Aron Lund, in his June 2011 monograph, *The Ghosts of Hama*, there was significant precedent to be found in the unrest that engulfed the country between 1976 and 1982:

> [By] the late 1970s, the Syrian economy was hurting from corruption and mismanagement, escalating military expenditures, and a withdrawal of foreign sponsorship. This caused shortages of goods and spiralling inflation, painful to the population at large, and perhaps particularly to the politicized middle classes.

> Meanwhile, Hafez el-Assad's political standing had been badly hurt by his reliance on Alawite sectarianism to control the security forces, by repeated clashes with Sunni fundamentalists (eg. in 1973, over the new constitution), by nepotism and corruption, and, last but not least, by his intervention in Lebanon in 1976. The move into Lebanon was perceived by secular nationalists and leftists as an attack on their Palestinian and Lebanese allies, in favor of rightist, Christian militias such as the Phalanges, while conservative Sunnis saw it as a conspiracy of minorities against their fellow Muslims. [sic]

However, certain characteristics that coloured past revolts and uprisings bore similarities to 2011. As the uprising continued to grow over the summer and autumn of 2011, marked sectarian lines were drawn up: minorities were unanimously behind the regime; on the streets, Sunni Muslims were being cut down by government guns. In the years before the French authorities left Syria in 1946 leaders of the Alawite state (1922-1936) implored the occupiers to stay. A petition signed by 450,000 Alawites, Christians and other minorities in September 1936 pleaded with the French not to leave, to protect these minorities from the "mortal danger" they feared from Sunnis who they believed were waiting to slaughter them.

But the Sunnis of Damascus, Aleppo and elsewhere never sought revenge.

On the street and in homes around Syria in 2011–12, there was little spoken of the country's past brushes with revolution. Syrians did not resort to history books for answers to their latest troubles and hopes. Though they employed the pre-Assad flag in thousands of demonstrations, activists right around the country very rarely referred to past revolutions, successful or otherwise. When demonstrators took to the streets they did not use rhetoric that might be interpreted as having historical resonance. Opposition leaders did not look to the past as a means of seeking out ways to defeat the Assad regime.

***

By his own admission, President Assad was not in control of the crackdown that by May 2012 saw almost 10,000 Syrians killed, according to the UN. His unofficial role was to speak to foreign newspapers, to give the odd scripted speech, to toe the line. Journalists interviewing Assad said regularly that he appeared to be a regular guy – a *Sunday Telegraph* journalist called him a geek to his face.

The government – which is separate to what we may refer to as the regime – positioned itself in an appearance of working on reforms; to all extents a charade. They would announce new media laws, committees were set up to study amending the constitution, ministers would sign new bills to help people. Elections and referendums were held. Furthermore, banning foreign journalists from entering Syria arguably backfired: the outside world went to the protestors' YouTube videos for pictures and ideas of what was taking place and as such, received a one-sided message. When international journalists were allowed access to Syria in January 2012 following Syria's agreement to the Arab League initiative, they saw there was in fact broad backing for Assad on the streets of Damascus. Western media outlets reported that there was support "for both sides" – they could not deny this when they witnessed pro-regime rallies, orchestrated by the state or not. By then, the FSA was active in numerous parts of the country, attacking government checkpoints and military build-ings. It was these militias the regime wanted the journalists to see, and perhaps this explains why they regime allowed journal-ists in at that point.

The security services, as in the past, were out of reach of any authority in Syria during the revolt. Indeed, the role of the *shabi-ha*, though little discussed in mainstream western media analysis (save for a 950-word piece by the BBC), was immensely important during the uprising. The gangs, the *shabiha* ('ghost' in Arabic), worked their way through the summer, at first stirring up sectari-an tension by shooting up Sunni and Christian neighbourhoods in the coastal city of Lattakia, and then by carrying out the torture and mutilation of dozens of protestors and activists. These gangs were the glue that stuck everything together. In them, the government had a failsafe element with which to sell their legitimacy to the Syrian population and to a paralysed international community. As they travelled the country in military trucks and vehicles, no one batted an eyelid and they could move around Syria under the guise of being security officers. For the regime it was per-fectly set up: it would unleash its own gangs on dissenting dis-tricts and immediately claim the killings and attacks to be the work of the foreign-backed armed gangs, not their own forces. The *shabiha* would assassinate leading academics from minority religions in Homs, for example, to drive fear into anyone from those groups who might be thinking of jumping ship to the side of the protestors.

In all likelihood – though I may not quote or present any hard evidence – the regime was responsible for the bombings in Da-mascus on 23 December and 6 January, in Aleppo on 10 Feb-ruary, and for the attack that killed the French journalist Gilles Jacquier in Homs on 11 January. Theirs was a foolproof plan – almost. No doubt at least part of the reason the regime worked so hard to sell the armed gangs idea was because it was responsi-ble for putting them on the streets of the countryside in the first place through several prisoner 'amnesties'. Perhaps the general prisoner amnesty announced on 15 January was granted out of necessity as the regime ran out of money to pay those already out wreaking havoc on the streets. For those who believed the regime's line that it was dealing with gangs and terrorists, the amnesty served as something both to fear and to be confused by.

We may never know who made the decision to plant and detonate bombs in Damascus, to shoot dead 120 soldiers in Jisr al-Shaghour in June 2011, to unleash these inhumane gangs charged with mutilating and torturing their fellow Syrians, though I doubt Bashar al-Assad did. What we can be sure of is that in a country where security is controlled so extensively by the state, these incidents did not occur without a very clear and direct order. Inside Maher al-Assad's palace on the top of a mountain in Dummar, a western suburb of Damascus, lit up by flashing fluorescent street lights, was where plans for the regime's crackdown probably took place. It was here that the president's brother and a small group of men following their own brand of 1970s *realpolitik*, reached the decision to shoot down protestors in Deraa in March 2011. To these men their actions were justified: if they gave in the country would fall to Muslim extremists; the people adored Bashar; it was their job to maintain security; that was the only way they could stay in power; that was the only way to keep their privilege; there was a foreign media conspiracy against Syria; Syria was strong.

There is little doubt that those in power – the ministers, the presidential advisers, even the *mukhabarat* on the street – are little more than a cabal of gangsters who, through pure guile and willingness to create fear, installed brutality over Syria. They are not well-read. They did not attend college. Their mindset of statesmanship is non-existent. They will fight to the last man on the premise that those coming to take their places (Sunni, simply because Syria has a predominately Sunni population) want to kill them for being Alawite. The notion that the Sunnis were coming to take over because some Alawites have used/misused their power was never a reality for them. They will not negotiate because the concept is alien to them in their every day lives, never mind in the game that is international politics.

The stories of the 'powerful men' who back the regime are legendary in Syria. I have heard from the sons and cousins of these 'powerful men'. They do not refer to Marxism as the way to economic and political riches, nor do they refer to an absence of democratic values to claim Syrians are not ready to rule themselves; instead, they proudly tell stories of how an uncle shot his way out of a carjacking on the highway between Lattakia and Aleppo and how "He got shot and is in hospital but he killed two of them." "I am from Qardaha and Obama is a donkey," a proud Makhlouf teenager told me in January 2012. They do not care if Syria falls into civil war. They do not care if the entire Syrian population is destroyed as long as they and the few close people around them survive. This is the mentality facing the protest movement and the international community. Not a new problem, no. But a complex one.

The politically sclerotic actions of the regime were numerous. The same day the newly-formed Political Parties Committee announced that eleven applications to establish political parties had been received, the Syrian parliament reconvened for a third, unconstitutional time. Despite the parliament's term having ended the previous March, it met again in May, August and October.

Twelve days after the regime announced a ban on all imports taxed at 5 per cent and over in September 2011, the law was reversed. International media reported business leaders forced the volte-face but when I interviewed several leading businessmen for an article for ForeignPolicy.com at the time, all agreed that the business community held no power over the regime chiefs. Reform of the laws governing the media, political parties and elections was announced as dozens died in the streets around the country.

The regime's doublespeak amounted to plain hypocrisy. In January 2012 it announced the release of thousands of Syrians arrested during the revolt who "did not have blood on their hands". State television broadcasted prisoners being released and thanking Bashar al-Assad for setting them free and professing their love and support for the president. But the authorities had previously stated that they had caught and detained armed gangs and terrorists – they said nothing of detaining peaceful protestors; why would they? Of course the idea was to appease the growing protest movement by setting free sons, brothers and fathers, and to persuade those Syrians sitting on the sidelines.

One of the most important questions is this: why did Bashar al-Assad change type so quickly and so brutally? Though many will disagree, I do not believe he is the butcher his father was to the extent that he made all decisions and ordered all military activities. One reason for the ferocity of the crackdown is the ingrained and long-standing power and status of the commanding members in the regime, the individuals versed in the Hafez al-Assad 1970s way of dealing with citizens' demands – the so-called 'Alawite Higher Council'.

The regime set a path to run both itself and the country into the ground. It would not give up an inch of Syrian soil. One would not exist without the other. 'Syria al-Assad' or nothing.

These seismic changes in Syrian life naturally engendered new hopes and fears.

My friend, Samir, offered a chilling perspective on the future of Syria, and of the wider region. Drinking coffee at a café in mid-September 2011, from nowhere he brought up the topic of Israel. He spoke with a ferociousness I had never heard from him in three-and-a-half years.

"Before all these revolutions started happening I used to say 'OK, well Israel is here in the region, it took Palestinian lands but what can we do now, they are here' but now, when I see the sheer will of the Arabs, I see and think that we can really achieve things. The only reason we were quiet before was because the dictators governing us would say 'stop!' and the Arab masses would stop out of fear. Now there is no fear. The Arabs will reclaim the land they took and end the state of Israel." He is animated.

"Israel is the cancer, the sore on this region. I am more positive about the future of Arabs now than ever."

At the time of writing, the story of Syria's popular revolt is far from concluding, though a pronounced change in the situation has emerged with the arming of groups opposed to the regime. The regime has proved adept at fighting back and convincing many in Syria it was right all along to blame 'armed gangs'. In spite of glaring incompetence, more than I have been surprised by its ability to carry out massive operations in several different parts of the country at once. But whatever the coming years hold, and despite the many deaths, the revolution has been good for Syria. It has shown the authorities that the country will not stand for the corruption, the informal arrests and, most of all – the culture of fear.

***

Jordan's King Abdullah said what most were thinking at an economic conference in Amman in October 2011: "No one has any idea what to do about Syria". He later became the first Arab head of state to publicly say Assad should step down. He was right – no one does know what to do about Syria. The struggle between a partially organised though divided opposition, backed up by the protestors, on the one hand, and the regime on the other, may continue for years, though one thing is for sure: toppling the Assad regime will not fix Syria's ills overnight.

As Brian Whitaker notes in his book, *What's Really Wrong with the Middle East*, "Freedom in depth requires a society of engaged citizens that is confident enough in its own strengths to examine its own failings openly and honestly." In Syria, people do not like to examine their failings. They don't like to look weak. They are all bosses or prophets.

A staffer at a private bank from Lattakia told me in 2010 that when his brother knocked down a pedestrian in a car accident on a Damascus street he fled the capital for a month while his family attempted to sort out the issue. His family paid money to the family of the deceased. The state was not involved in this aspect of governance and the brother faced no legal judgment for his crime. Law and justice are realms so weak, corrupt and disingenuous in the state system that Syrians have rejected them in serious matters; they are forced to govern themselves; they can place no trust in the state.

"Syrians think in tribes," one man told me. "When we get a new government, under Assad or not, little will change. We will get a new mayor in our town; he will surround himself with his family and friends. His nieces and nephews will come to him looking for favours and jobs and he will give them what they want because he knows they can help guarantee his position. So even if these relatives are not experienced or suitable for the positions they ask for, they'll still get them. This goes all the way up to the top family."

There is some undeniable truth to this downbeat perspective. In almost any aspect of Syrian life a man who gets a new job will see his younger brother come to his place of work and ask him for money. With time, he will ask his boss if there is a job for his brother, then his cousin and so forth. Simply put, those in positions of power are expected to aid those nearest them.

However, to call this tribalism is incorrect because the regime's governance, or lack thereof, bears primary responsibility for such social patterns. It has succeeded in sowing seeds of fear among businessmen and other groups to the extent that the only individuals that business people and entrepreneurs can trust are their blood relatives. For this reason Syrian business remains dominated by family conglomerates, as it was a hundred years ago. Furthermore, the gap between state and society, which transpires through a general sentiment that nothing associated with the state can be productive for the private individual feeds this deficit, this hole, that the state is supposed to fill but does not and cannot.

The state does little for the average Syrian; there is no connection between the two other than the periodic jumping through bureaucratic hoops the latter must endure when dealing with officialdom. If a Syrian crashes his or her car they will not report it to the police as the authorities will do nothing to help. So what must Syrians do to ensure the welfare of themselves and their families? They must build themselves up using their families.

The culture of obscurantism that plagues Syrian society has made and will continue to make change in Syria more difficult. But this, a country with such a prominent oral culture, may find talking the only way to bridge the now deep-seated differences between religious communities and between those who support and oppose the regime. Responsibility and reconciliation among Syrians themselves will be the key factors in deciding whether Syria's future is bright or not, though the signs are not positive.

The revolt has also left Syrians facing an identity crisis. Before the revolt, they were a people who lived under the perception that they were the 'other' in the international political scene. They were pro-Hezbollah and pro-Iran. They were anti-Saudi Arabia and anti-America.

The freedom-advocating and democratic western world stood against Syrians when Israel stole the Golan Heights in 1967 and when it marched on Damascus in 1973. When American troops crossed into Syrian territory in late October 2008 and killed seven people Syrians were rightly livid. The regime co-opted this by organising a huge anti-America rally a day later where Bashar was the focus, not the Americans. Syrians have sided with Palestinians out of moral duty (and because of the regime's propaganda), but they are treated as outcasts when looking for work in the Gulf as thousands do every year. Most Syrians cannot get even tourist visas for Europe or North America. In the midst of the revolt many Gulf countries also stopped issuing visas for Syrians.

Today they are faced with major conflicts of conscience. They have a degree of freedom of speech not permitted in public for decades and many are unsure how to react to this. The vast majority that make up Syria's young population are on the cusp of something they have never experienced, and only seen through the prism of a television set or the internet. Moreover, where do Syrians stand regarding Hamas, Hezbollah and Iran? For decades these entities served to unite Syrians, now the very opposite is the case – some protestors burned Hezbollah flags and effigies of Hassan Nasrallah because the Lebanese group sided with the regime over the protestors. There is an identity yet to be formed as to what the Syrian people stand for, and where they want to go as a country which cuts across ethnic and sectarian lines.

Syrians like to cast blame, be they civilians or regime officials. But responsibility and respect for the rule of law – even as the foundations of such principles flounder – are essential in staving off civil conflict.

The regime's associates have not led by example. When will the army and police stop discolouring the registration numbers of their cars (so as to avoid speed cameras) as they did for the duration of the unrest? When will those driving cars with blackened windows stop racing past the rest of the general public, showing off in plain view how they enjoy privileges others don't? When will they stop at traffic lights and park in designated areas? When will they pay their bills and not use their security 'credentials' to commandeer petrol and alcohol? They are foremost amongst those calling for the regime to stay, though they flash their car lights to get cars out of their way on the streets, only to pull into shops to buy alcoholic soft drinks (as I have witnessed). They may think they are almighty, but the rest of the country is watching, and watching with growing anger.

Naturally, the opposition and protestors cannot be absolved of sin. The Free Syria Army and other elements acting under its name have killed randomly. True, they were pressured into such actions during the spring and summer of 2011, but the pre-meditated targeting of soldiers and security officers thereafter were acts of terrorism, however desperate, not acts of war. Besides, strategically it was a dreadful move, serving to legitimise the regime's claims that it was fighting armed gangs since the very beginning of the revolt. From Burhan Ghalioun to Abdulrahman the car mechanic (see Chapter IV), people called for the fall of the regime, but what then? It appears the car mechanic had as much a clue what to do next as Ghalioun.

Hasan, a friend who manages a café in Baramkeh in central Damascus, told me of one incident that made him turn against the protest movement, though he hated the regime.

"Last night I took a taxi home and on the way there was a man and woman who waved the taxi down. The woman was on the verge of giving birth. So we picked them up and we drove on to Melaha, where I lived and where she would get medical assistance. On the way, we came across a demonstration. The protestors would not let our taxi go through. 'You are a spy for the regime' they shouted at the taxi driver. 'I'm just trying to get this woman to the hospital – look at her!' responded the driver. But no, they would not let us through. They kept saying we were coming as spies for the regime, for the security. What spies were we?! The woman was about to have a baby and I was going home from work! We had to turn around and go back."

It is Syrians like Hasan that the regime and the opposition need to appeal to – the silent majority simply seeking a better life. Instead he and millions of others are undecided in their views. Ask Syrians who Ayman Abdel Noor – the editor-in-chief of the reformist website AllForSyria and a Baathist who resided in Dubai during the unrest – is and they will look at you blankly. Moreover, those who took to the streets in the spring of 2011 did not do so championing democracy. They did so because their fathers, brothers and sons disappeared, were beaten or were killed. They had no links to America, Israel or other enemies of Syria. They were not members of the political opposition.

As a result, the state of flux between revolt and civil conflict will likely continue for the foreseeable future. If the regime or the opposition could win over such individuals they would surely have enough support to bring down the other. But neither side has, nor do they appear likely to do so.

On the other hand, is there truth to the idea that Syrians, because of their complete lack of freedom, need to be ruled with a firm hand from the top down?

What happened when the police stopped coming around every afternoon to stop people illegally selling trinkets on the side of the streets? Mass illegal stalls were set up. What happened when traffic police were temporarily taken away from their traffic light posts or when speed cameras were switched off? People sped through red lights and failed to obey speed limits, resulting in accidents and injuries. What took place when government officials were not around to control illegal house-building? Civilians fired up outhouses and home extensions without seeking expertise or state permission. And when government employees don't visit cafés every day to ensure there is no smoking in line with the 2010 law? People smoked even more openly. Can the police or the government or Bashar al-Assad be blamed for these failures to respect the law?

The international narrative on the revolt in Syria has been decidedly one-sided. Why did no police or security stop the protest in Jdaydieh Artouz that cold January night? Did the security stay away because they were overstretched? It was certainly not reported in the international media and for me to pitch a story talking about such restraint to Europe or the US would have found me promptly declined. In the town of Qatana, close by, some locals said the army only entered in July 2011 after shops had been destroyed and civil authority broke down following clashes between local Sunnis and Alawites. Did the army lock-down this town simply to restore order, or because the protes-tors were violent gangs?

The day will come when the regime falls and Syrians will need to take responsibility for their actions and to admit wrongdoing. Otherwise their country will fall down around them. It will not simply be: "Why are you driving through the red light?" It will be "Why are you shooting at that Sunni house?" The repercussions of Syrians themselves not soon coming to terms with the issue of responsibility could be disastrous for the long-term future of the country. Only Syrians themselves can answer these ques-tions and stabilise their futures, no matter how much blame they cast around.

ACKNOWLEDGEMENTS

This book, and my understanding of Syria, have their roots in the stories of those I have lived with and met since 2007. It took years rather than months to build up an understanding of what led some Syrians into revolt and others to essentially ignore the movement for change. For these reasons, my thanks go primarily to the Syrians who agreed to meet me and lay out their thoughts and fears when often it was safer to simply say "no".

I have attempted to bring to light here the stories of shopkeepers, businessmen, school teachers, mechanics, doctors, students and state employees; they are the heart and soul of this book. I hope to have done them justice, and that this account helps them recognise and overcome their own divisions. Few of their names are recorded, but their fears and angers most definitely are. For your time, energy and courage, I thank you all.

Thanks to my wife, who endured much more than just an absent spouse as this book was written.

To Stephen and Teresa for never holding me back and for supporting me in seeing Syria through for as long as I could, I thank you both.

This book also owes a great deal to Joseph Burke who carefully read early drafts, offered questions and constructive criticism, and whose judgement and clarity of thought dispelled many of my own concerns and misgivings.

Thanks also to: Sari Akminas, Abdulghani Attar, Bassel Bannoud, Sydma Damasceno, Obeida Hamad, Malek Jandali, Aron Lund, Ola Malas, Sami Moubayed, John O'Brennan, Michael Provence, Ghaleb Saad, Eiad Shurbaji, John Wreford and Jihad Yazigi.

Sections of the reporting that appears in this book were published in newspapers and magazines in Ireland, Jordan, Syria, the United Kingdom and the United States. Thanks to Richard Beeston, Cory Eldridge, Pete Gelling, Martha Kearns, David Kenner, Roula Khalaf, Pat Lancaster, Sami Moubayed, Peter Murtagh and Griff Witte for allowing me to record in *Revolt* parts of the work that appeared in their newspapers and magazines.

Finally, thanks to Michael Dwyer and all at Hurst.

Any errors in the text are my own.

FURTHER READING

Cockburn, Patrick, "The attempt to topple President Assad has failed," *The Independent*, 25 March 2012.

"The Squeeze on Assad," *The Economist*, 30 June, 2011.

Fahim, Kareem, "Sharp rise in violence halts monitoring by League in Syria," *The New York Times*, 28 January 2012.

Harling, Peter and Sarah Birke, "Beyond the fall of the Syrian regime," Middle East Research and Information Project, 24 February 2012.

International Crisis Group, "The Syrian People's Slow-motion Revolution," 6 July 2011.

———, "The Syrian Regime's Slow-motion Suicide,"13 July 2011.

———, "Uncharted Waters: Thinking Through Syria's Dynamics," 24 November 2011.

International Crisis Group, "Now or Never: A Negotiated Transition for Syria," 5 March 2012.

Khouri, Rami G., Agence Global, "One year on in Syria," 19 March 2012.

Landis, Joshua, "Syrians must win the revolution on their own," *Foreign Policy*, 9 August 2011.

Lesch, David W., "The President I know," *The New York Times*, 29 March 2011.

Lund, Aron, "The Ghosts of Hama: The Bitter Legacy of Syria's Failed 1979-82 Revolution," Swedish International Liberal Centre, June 2011.

"Why Civil War is Unlikely — After Assad," *Near East Quarterly*, November 2011.

Pipes, Daniel, "The Alawi capture of power," *Middle Eastern Studies*, vol. 25 no. 4, 1989.

Rosen, Nir, "Assad's Alawites: An entrenched community," Al Jazeera, 12 October 2011.

"President Assad's speech to the new government," SANA, 18 April 2011.

Shadid, Anthony, "In scarred Syria City, a vision of a life free from dictators," *The New York Times*, 19 July 2011.

Sly, Liz ,"Syria's Zabadani is 'liberated,' but for how long?" *The Washington Post*, 21 January 2012.

Starr, Stephen, "Five Years in Damascus," ForeignPolicy.com, 29 February 2012.

——— ,"Mass killings uncovered near Damascus," GlobalPost, 3 February, 2012.

SyriaComment, "Western press misled – Who shot the nine soldiers in Banyas? Not Syrian security forces," 13 April 2011.

———, "Will sanctions bring down the Syrian regime?," 15 November 2011.

Books

Lawson, Fred H. (ed.), *Demystifying Syria: SOAS Middle East Issues Series*, London: Saqi Books, 2010.

Provence, Michael, *The Great Syrian Revolt and the Rise of Arab Nationalism*, Austin, TX: University of Texas Press, 2005.

Seale, Patrick, *Asad: The Struggle for the Middle East*, Berkeley, CA: University of California Press, 1990.

Tejel, Jordi, *Syria's Kurds: History, Politics and Society*, London: Routledge, 2008.

Whitaker, Brian, *What's Really Wrong with the Middle East*, London: Saqi Books, 2010.

Wieland, Carsten, *Syria at Bay: Secularism, Islamism and 'Pax Americana'*, London: Hurst, 2005.

INDEX